Quarterly Essay

Quarterly Essay is published four times a year by Black Inc., an imprint of Schwartz Media Pty Ltd. Publisher: Morry Schwartz.

ISBN 978-1-86395-681-9 ISSN 1832-0953

Subscriptions – 1 year (4 issues): $59 within Australia incl. GST. Outside Australia $89. 2 years (8 issues): $105 within Australia incl. GST. Outside Australia $165.

Payment may be made by Mastercard or Visa, or by cheque made out to Schwartz Media. Payment includes postage and handling.

To subscribe, fill out and post the subscription card or form inside this issue, or subscribe online:

www.quarterlyessay.com
subscribe@blackincbooks.com
Phone: 61 3 9486 0288

Correspondence should be addressed to:

The Editor, Quarterly Essay
37–39 Langridge Street
Collingwood VIC 3066 Australia
Phone: 61 3 9486 0288 / Fax: 61 3 9486 0244
Email: quarterlyessay@blackincbooks.com

Editor: Chris Feik. Management: Sophy Williams, Caitlin Yates. Publicity: Anna Lensky. Design: Guy Mirabella. Assistant Editor: Kirstie Innes-Will. Production Coordinator: Siân Scott-Clash. Typesetting: Duncan Blachford.

Nhanaburru, wangkanmala bapurru dhimirrunguru, arnhemland, nganaburrungu ngurrngu dilak mala, nganthun yukurra nhuna 26th Prime Minister Australia-wu. Nhukala ganydjarr'yu nhunhi nhe ngurrungu walalangu malangura nhuma walala rrambangi, Australian Parliament-ngura, ga ngurrungu Dharuk-mirri nhangu Garraywu Queen Elizabeth-gu, yurru nhandarryun-marama djinawa-lili Australian-dhu luku-wu rom-dhu yurru dharangan ga galmuma nganapurrungu dhangang ga bukmak nha-mala nhanapurrungu:

- Nhanapurrungu walnga-mirri dhukarry ngudhudal-yana.
- Nhanapurrungu, wanga, wanga-ngaraka ga nguy gapu, ngunhi dhimirrunguru, arnhemland.
- Dharrima gungnharra, warkthunara, lukunydja rrupiya-yu wanga-wuy-ga gapu-wuy ga dhangangnha-yana ga lukunydjana yana.
- Dharray walnga-wuy ga djaka yurru nhanapurrung-gala-nguwu djamarrkuli-wu yalalangu-wu.

Dhuwalanydja rom dhuwalana bilina.

Dhuwalanydja rom wawungu wanga-wuy ngandarryunmarama Australian-gala bapurrulili.

Nganapurru marrliliyama nhukula ngurru-warryun-narayngu, marr yurru Commonwealth Parliament ngurru warrwun ga dharangan dhuwala rom ga marryuwak gumana dhayutakumana lukunydja rom.

— Yolngu Petition, 2008
(English translation on page 2)

A RIGHTFUL PLACE | Race, recognition and a more complete commonwealth

Noel Pearson

Had Galarrwuy Yunupingu and his dilak elders been present at the creation of the Commonwealth of Australia in 1901, there might have been a scene like this:

> I wait for the new prime minister ... An event is taking place at Yirrkala and I have called the leaders of the 13 clans together. No children or young people will participate, only leaders, men and women who have proved themselves: dilak. By my side are Djinyini Gondarra and the leaders of the Elcho clans, Richard Ganduwuy and Dunga Dunga Gondarra, Butharripi Gurruwiwi. Wilson Ganambarr, Gali Gurruwiwi, Gekurr Guyula and Timmy Burrawanga are there. Laklak and Dhuwarrwarr Marika are there, too, along with the great old man from Gan Gan, Garrawan Gumana. My cousin Banambi Wunungmurra brings the prime minister down to us. We have a petition for him.

Learning of the cataclysmic history experienced by Aboriginal tribes in the coastal south and east of the country and the inexorable expansion into the west and the north in the first 110 years of European colonisation, and fearing the time when the Yolngu of Arnhem Land would face the same devastation, Yunupingu might have presented Edmund Barton – along with Sir Samuel Griffith and the other founding fathers of the new nation – with a petition, as he did Kevin Rudd in 2008:

> We, the united clans of East Arnhem land, through our most senior dilak, do humbly petition you, the ... Prime Minister of Australia, in your capacity as the first amongst equals in the Australian Parliament, and as the chief adviser to Her Majesty ... to secure within the Australian Constitution the recognition and protection of our full and complete right to:
>
> - Our way of life in all its diversity;
> - Our property, being the lands and waters of East Arnhem land;
> - Economic independence, through the proper use of the riches of our land and waters in all their abundance and wealth;
> - Control of our lives and responsibility for our children's future.

In going to the heart of the matter of constitutional recognition, there are few more important documents than Yunupingu's December 2008 essay in the Monthly, which discusses the Yolngu Petition.

It is no mere essay. It is an existential prayer.

A prayer on behalf of a people fearing their future non-existence. Fear that the old trajectory of colonisation and its continuation in the new nation will lead to the disappearance of Yolngu from history.

I read this document and hear the voices of William Cooper, Bill Ferguson and Jack Patten echoing down the century, the voices of Vincent Lingiari, Charlie Perkins and Eddie Mabo. I sense the Day of Mourning in 1938 and the establishment of the Tent Embassy in 1972. I hear the voices of Margaret Tucker, Faith Bandler and Lowitja O'Donoghue.

My thoughts flash back to the warriors who fought the colonial invasion: Yagan, Pemulwuy, Windradyne, Jundamurra.

I cannot take my mind off William Lanne, the so-called "Last Man" of Tasmania.

In talking about Yunupingu's existential fears for the future of his people in the deepest, hottest north, I want to re-remember what happened in the deepest, coldest south of the country, at the beginning of two centuries of Australian history. Because I think that as the old Tasmanians saw their world destroyed and felt history's determination that they should disappear from the earth, they faced the same fears.

Yunupingu enjoyed a youth in the classical culture of the Yolngu ("My father sent me to school, although he worried that I might lose my Gumatj identity"). He was educated by Methodist missionaries ("As I received my education from my clan leaders and from the balanda teachers, I watched as the world changed"), and, although he attended Bible college for two years, he returned to the traditions of his people ("I dedicated myself, under the direction of my father and the older men, to a Yolngu future").

In his essay, Yunupingu touches on every prime minister since Gough Whitlam. He recalls taking the newly elected Malcolm Fraser on a fishing trip: "I try and put words in his mind about the importance of land, about the importance of respect, about giving things back in a proper way, not a halfway thing," but the prime minister is preoccupied with catching barramundi – "he's not listening; he doesn't have to."

He recalls how Bob Hawke's promises of a treaty turned to tears of regret when his last act as prime minister was to hang the Barunga Statement in Parliament House ("I am sure that his tears are for his own failure – we have no treaty; his promise was hollow and he has not delivered").

The prime ministerial and ministerial merry-go-round over the decades lends a depressing circularity to Yunupingu's long history of dealing with power in Australia:

> I have walked the corridors of power; I have negotiated and cajoled and praised and begged prime ministers and ministers, travelled the world and been feted; I have opened the doors to men of power

and prestige; I have had a place at the table of the best and the brightest in the Australian nation – and at times success has seemed so close, yet it always slips away.

He cares nothing for his association with power but only for the purpose to which he wishes to direct it, for his purpose is pressing: "And behind me, in the world of my father, the Yolngu world is always under threat, being swallowed up by whitefellas."

The existential angst of the tribal leader who fears for the future of his people is harrowing ("it is a pressure that I feel now every moment of my life – it frustrates me and drives me crazy; at night it is like a splinter in my mind").

Yunupingu recalls meeting minister Mal Brough at his Dhanaya home-land in the wake of the Northern Territory Intervention ("we talked as men should – about the future of children and of failures and frustrations, and how we could turn it all around with action") and raises the question of constitutional recognition ("to bring my people in from the cold, bring us into the nation").

The future is the source of Yunupingu's psychic trouble:

> I care for and protect my clan. But I have not mastered the future. I find that I now spend my days worrying about how I can protect the present from the future. I feel the future moving in on the Yolngu world, the Gumatj world, like an inevitable tide, except every year the tide rises further, moving up on us, threatening to drown us under the water, unable to rise again. The water sands under our feet shift and move so often – the land to which we can reach out is often distant, unknown.

Yunupingu's achievements in his struggle for land rights were colossal, both for his people and for people across the Northern Territory and the continent. There is no doubt that securing a territorial base for Yolngu people has gone a long way towards underpinning that society. But Yun-upingu's assessment of his life's work is bleak:

I look back now on a lifetime of effort and I see that we have not moved very far at all. For all the talk, all the policy, all the events, all the media spectaculars and fine speeches, the gala dinners, what has been achieved? I have maintained the traditions, kept the law, performed my role – yet the Yolngu world is in crisis; we have stood still. I look around me and I feel the powerlessness of all our leaders.

And the gulf between the powers-that-be in Canberra and the Yolngu world is as vast as ever:

> There is no one in power who has the experience to know these things. There is not one federal politician who has any idea about the enormity of the task. And how could they? Who in the senior levels of the commonwealth public service has lived through these things? Who in the parliament? No one speaks an Aboriginal language, let alone has the ability to sit with a young man or woman and share that person's experience and find out what is really in their heart. They have not raised these children in their arms, given them everything they have, cared for them, loved them, nurtured them. They have not had their land stolen, or their rights infringed, or their laws broken. They do not bury the dead as we bury our dead.

To understand what Yunupingu is talking about here is to understand how misguided it is to reduce the indigenous predicament in Australia to the banal idea of "closing the gap" on indigenous disadvantage. There is something more fundamental at stake: whether the Yolngu of Arnhem Land will find a place in the Australian nation so that – honouring their fathers and mothers, as obliged by the Second Commandment – they may live long on the earth.

It is a predicament shared by the Wik and the Yidinji of Queensland. By the Wiradjuri of central New South Wales and the Bundjalung of the Northern Rivers district. By the Kaurna of South Australia and the Anangu of central Australia. The Nyungar and Martu of Western Australia. By the Kulin nation and the Yorta Yorta of Victoria. By the Ngunnawal of the capital and by William Lanne's Palawa descendants in Tasmania.

This is a problem of the world. The planet is occupied by thousands of distinct ethnic groupings, with their own languages and cultures and territorial connections. Many are indigenous to the territories in which they live. Depending on how these distinct peoples are defined, they number between 7000 and 10,000.

But if the fragmentation of Babel resulted in this great diversity, the Age of Imperialism and the creation of empires scrambled many of these societies. Globalisation and modernity now force blending, assimilation and integration, and rupture the isolation and containment that enabled diverse peoples to maintain their esoteric identities, cultures and languages. There has been much history in this process. And that has necessarily left legacies of grievance.

Settler colonialism is one such history, replete with grievance the world over, not least in our country.

There are four focuses of grievance: identity as a people; the territorial lands of a people; language; and culture. Peoples hold hard to these four things.

And then there are the nation-states that harbour peoples. There are only 200 or so of them.

So the problem of the world is: how do 10,000 distinct peoples live well and prosper – and get along with each other – within 200 nation-states?

There is surely no future in hoping the nation-states will further fragment, so that more nations can be created which reflect the existential convictions of distinct peoples. The existing nation-states, jealously guarding their integrity, have no appetite for further fragmentation. At best, in the future, new states of Palestine and a self-governing West Papua will emerge.

But it is also surely clear that nation-states denying the existence of distinct peoples within their territories and insisting upon the integrity of the unitary state, without recognition of distinct peoples and cultures, is no solution either. Insisting on comprehensive assimilation as the concomitant of nationalism is not the recipe for unity within nations; it foments too much ethnic destruction and resistance.

There is an alternative to fragmentation and the assimilatory state. It is recognition and reconciliation: where peoples within nation-states come to terms with each other and commit to the nation, while respecting the existential anxieties of distinct peoples.

The Constitution of Australia adopted in 1901 afforded no such recognition. It is this recognition which Yunupingu seeks on behalf of his people, and in doing so he asks a question that remains unanswered after two centuries: is there a proper and rightful place for the original peoples of Australia in the nation created from their ancestral lands?

The inspiration for *The War of the Worlds* came one day when Wells and his brother Frank were strolling through the peaceful countryside in Surrey, south of London. They were discussing the invasion of the Australian island of Tasmania in the early 1800s by European settlers, who hunted down and killed most of the primitive people who lived there. To emphasise the reaction of these people, Frank said, "Suppose some beings from another planet were to drop out of the sky suddenly and begin taking over Surrey and then all of England!"

– Malvina G. Vogel, "Foreword" (2005)

to H.G. Wells, *The War of the Worlds*

A personal quadrant of the Australian landscape

I came upon this foreword some years ago when sharing an enthusiasm of my youth for H.G. Wells' *The War of the Worlds* with my young son. Even as he makes his way through his own all-consuming passions of boyhood – Thomas, the Crocodile Hunter, *Pirates of the Caribbean*, *Lord of the Rings*, Minecraft and now Harry Potter – I indulge my own nostalgia by sharing those things that possessed me when I was a boy. We've done *Richard III*, to which we will doubtless return. We've read Charles Portis's masterpiece *True Grit*, and watched the original John Wayne film and the Coen brothers' remake a hundred times. We've acted out the shoot-out scenes; he's always Rooster. We are yet to get to Sir Arthur Conan Doyle and *The Hound of the Baskervilles*. His younger sister and I have started *Great Expectations*.

First turned on by Jeff Wayne's musical version of *The War of the Worlds* in early high school, aware of Orson Welles' radio hoax and having read the Wells book, I was stunned to have been unaware of the inspiration for the idea of a Martian invasion of England – its origin in what was called the "extirpation" of the original Tasmanians. I was disquieted that the source of this extraordinary production in world culture was unknown to me. I knew it was likely unknown to everyone around me, and to almost all of my fellow Australians. How come?

H.G. Wells knew of the original Tasmanians, but that did not mean he felt empathy for the fate of this "inferior race" at the hands of the British. Instead he subscribed to the scientific racism of his era, believing them "Palaeolithic," and writing, "The Tasmanians, in spite of their human likeness, were entirely swept out of existence in a war of extermination waged by European immigrants."

In *The Last Man: A British Genocide in Tasmania* (2014), the English historian Tom Lawson shows how the destruction of the Tasmanians played out in British culture. We will return to Lawson's contribution to the debate on genocide in Tasmania soon, after we lift the scales from our eyes concerning some of the most revered figures of that culture in the nineteenth century.

The novelist Anthony Trollope, in his emigration guide *Australia and New Zealand*, demanded his British readers squarely face the fact that colonisation involved the theft of land and the destruction of its original owners — which fact was not morally wrong but an advancement of civilisation. Lawson writes that Trollope cannot be taken as other than calling for genocide when he wrote: "of the Australian black man we may say certainly that he has to go. That he should perish without unnecessary suffering should be the aim of all who are concerned in this matter."

Charles Darwin, the century's greatest scientist (whom Lawson calls "a self-conscious liberal humanitarian"), while opposing polygenist theories that various races were distinct species, nevertheless proposed culture as the basis of inferiority and superiority (Lawson: "indigenous Tasmanians in Darwin's formulation had been swept aside by a more culturally developed, more civilised people"). Lawson writes: "*The Descent of Man* was Darwin's answer to that new political context, in which he asserted that while biologically the human race *was* singular there were in effect cultural differences that allowed for some form of racial hierarchy. The Tasmanians appeared at the bottom of this hierarchy."

Darwin wrote:

> when civilised nations come into contact with barbarians the struggle is short ... Of the causes which lead to the victory of civilised nations, some are plain and simple, others complex and obscure. We can see that the cultivation of the land be fatal in many ways to savages, for they cannot, or will not, change their habits.

Of course, the deformation of Darwin's theory of natural selection into social Darwinism and the scientific racism of the latter half of the nineteenth century and the first half of the twentieth was the source of much misery for indigenes throughout the colonial world. Darwin was not entirely innocent of this conflation of biology and culture, which gave scientific authority to an ideology of inevitability about the demise of the Tasmanians and others of their ilk in the face of European superiority.

I expected Charles Darwin. But I didn't expect Charles Dickens.

Of the century's greatest English novelist, the author of *Great Expectations* and an immortal canon, Lawson writes, "Dickens famously attacked ... the humanitarian idealisation of the 'noble savage' in June 1853, in a furious denunciation that amounts, to use modern-day language, to a call for genocide."

Dickens wrote:

> I call him a savage, and I call a savage something highly desirable to be civilised off the face of the earth ... my position is that if we have anything to learn from the Noble Savage, it is what to avoid. His virtues are a fable; his happiness is a delusion; his nobility nonsense. We have no greater justification for being cruel to the miserable object, than for being cruel to a William Shakespeare or an Isaac Newton; but he passes away before an immeasurably better and higher power than ever ran wild in any earthly woods, and the world will be all the better when his place knows him no more.

I am yet to work out whether, how and when to tell my girl that the creator of Pip, Pumblechook and that convict wretch Magwitch may have wished her namesake great-great-grandmother off the face of the earth.

Ironically, when one's identification with the magnificent literary treasures of England turns out so, there is a Dickensian pathos to the crestfallen scene. One is acutely conscious of what Robert Hughes called "anachronistic moralising," but the bridge between our contemporary values and those of Dickens' time should surely be a universal and timeless humanity – but alas not.

I don't know whether it is hard for all Aborigines, but it certainly is for me, to read this history with a historian's dispassionate objectivity and without the emotional convulsions of identification and memory. As a child, I loved my mother's mother most in the world; her humour, generosity and ill-temper I often detect in myself and in the various countenances of my children. An irascible, pipe-smoking, bush-born lady, she bustled with her portmanteau on perambulations to her numerous grandchildren growing up in the Daintree and Bloomfield missions, and the Hope Vale Mission of my childhood. She could have been Truganini, but less travelled and from a smaller rainforest world than the nineteenth-century Tasmanian whose passing in 1876 was a world-historical event, marking the assumed extinction of a race. It was a reverberation I would feel when I learnt her name in primary school and the awful meaning of her distinction.

How many Australians born in the 138 years since Truganini's death learnt her legend and scarcely thought deeper about the enormity of the loss she represented, and the history that led to it? Her spirit casts a long shadow over Australian history, but we have nearly all of us found a way to avert our eyes from its meaning.

That small item in the primary-school curriculum of my childhood would have been learnt by all my generation. Maybe it wasn't a formal part of any syllabus, but it was one of those salient facts of Australian society that every child absorbed, like Don Bradman's batting average and

Phar Lap's outsized heart. It would have been learnt by John Howard and Paul Keating. By Gough Whitlam and Robert Menzies. I don't know if they teach kids about Truganini today.

As a student of history but not a historian, I am as well read as many, but I too have skirted this history. Learning later in life of the descendants of the original Tasmanians, and the offence of the assumption of extinction, seemed to lessen the imperative to face the question of Truganini's moral legacy. Maybe the scale of the horror diminished as the country accepted the fact of the continued survival of Tasmania's Aboriginal community. But surely the fact of the descendants' survival does not in any way alter or diminish the profundity of what happened to their ancestors.

In his 1968 Boyer Lecture, W.E.H. Stanner spoke of the "Great Australian Silence":

> inattention on such a scale cannot possibly be explained by absent-mindedness. It is a structural matter, a view from a window which has been carefully placed to exclude a whole quadrant of the landscape. What may have begun as a simple forgetting of other possible views turned under habit and over time into something like a cult of forgetfulness practised on a national scale. We have been able for so long to disremember the Aborigines that we are now hard put to keep them in mind even when we most want to do so.

This excluded quadrant of the landscape was not just a national phenomenon: it was personal. Forgetfulness was not just a cult: it was resorted to by individual Australians, descendants of both the invading Europeans and the Aborigines. Australians who, like me, struggle to work out how we might deal with the past.

The cult of forgetfulness

I had hoped to avoid the past – for sheerly political reasons. In this essay I seek to make a case for constitutional reform recognising indigenous Australians. This must by definition be a unifying cause. If we don't have an argument that can persuade 90 per cent of the nation, then the cause of constitutional reform is lost. Any successful case must transcend the natural political and cultural polarities of Australian society, and seek and seize political bipartisanship. This can only happen if Australians faced with a constitutional proposition are led by the better angels of our nature.

The risk with history is that it may provoke partisanship and division, both among the cultural and political tribes of the nation at large, and between indigenous and non-indigenous Australians.

We witnessed this in the History Wars of the 1990s and 2000s, when the "black armband" historians and political leaders were pitted against the "white blindfold" historians and political leaders. Led by Keith Windschuttle on the one hand and Robert Manne and Henry Reynolds on the other, the wars were a bitter and not always illuminating affair.

But the wars were unavoidable.

Following the Great Australian Silence at the end of the 1960s, from the '70s through to the '90s there was a burgeoning of Aboriginal history, led by scholars such as Reynolds. In hindsight, given the intense relationship between indigenous policy and politics and the representation and interpretation of the nation's history, the rise of a counter-narrative in the form of Windschuttle's *The Fabrication of Aboriginal History* (Volume 1, 2002), was inevitable. No discourse can lean one way for long. No wind can blow from one direction without restraint.

The public contributions of the doyen of conservative historians, Geoffrey Blainey, were the first indications of the discomfort of those who held the settler Australian narrative. Blainey would have been better qualified to steady the ship of the nation's narrative had he done so as a historian. Instead he did so as a polemicist. His caricaturing of the new frontier history as the "black armband" view made for a tribal fight in the public square, rather than a debate within the discipline of history. Blainey's commendable record on Aboriginal history was obscured in the ensuing debate: he was not contemptuous of the Aborigines; he wanted to defend settler traditions. It was most unfortunate that Blainey made his case in this manner. A serious point in an unserious way.

Over the past three decades, I have read Henry Reynolds' numerous books, and I well understand the grounds upon which conservative and nationalist readers of his histories baulk at his interpretations. It seems to me that Reynolds' lifelong contribution has been a liberal pursuit of a shared history for the nation. He has been about finding grace for the nation by breaking the silence on Aboriginal history and all the time being faithful to Australia.

But there are two problems with Reynolds' project. First, he comes to the case from a patently political background. His wife, Margaret, was a Labor senator for Queensland during the Hawke years, and the couple came at politics and indigenous issues from a certain Labor left perspective. There is a strongly Fabian tone to his arguments, and trenchant advocacy frames his books. In the acknowledgments of *An Indelible Stain? The Question of Genocide in Australian History* (2001), Reynolds tellingly reveals: "My family – Margaret, John, Anna and Rebecca – have been, as ever, supportive and have frequently reinforced my commitment to progress along the often difficult road of human rights advocacy." Which, for his critics, raises the question whether he was primarily engaged in academic history or human rights advocacy, and perhaps suggests that more dispassion and less politics might have better enabled Reynolds to secure a shared history for his fellow Australians.

I will say at this point that I am at one with Henry and Margaret Reynolds on the human rights side of the equation, but at odds with them on the responsibilities side. They have been and are mute on the social crisis of Aboriginal Australia; indeed, I have observed that the policies needed to tackle indigenous misery – economic integration, social order and welfare reform – have been championed by the right, and in 2006 noted that "Windschuttle and [Gary] Johns are more attuned to many of the necessary policies than the progressives."

The same thing struck me about rock star and former Labor politician Peter Garrett as the former senator Reynolds. No greater friends when it came to indigenous rights and paying the rent and decrying the burning beds of history, but completely silent about the unravelling social crisis of the present – and, to the extent they thought about what needed to be done, mostly wrongheaded. It is strange that people who would insist strongly on Aboriginal agency in the past would turn a blind eye to such passivity in the present.

Second, I find persuasive Bain Attwood's critique of Reynolds' oeuvre as consisting overmuch of "juridical history": the telling of history as if presenting evidence in a legal case before a court. I share Attwood's view that Reynolds' core trilogy – The Other Side of the Frontier (1981), Frontier (1987) and With the White People (1990) – is unimpeachable. But much of the rest has the features of juridical history, and too many contentions seem to be submissions to a court case rather than based on a proper grappling with the political economy of the time and circumstances of which he writes. Therefore some appear thin.

In a 2007 essay for Griffith REVIEW, I analysed the dynamic of the political discourse between progressives and conservatives. I observed that the conservative camp comprised a broad spectrum, ranging from true denialists such as Windschuttle to those who, in their cups, would admit the truths of Aboriginal history, but who were defensive of their own heritage and of the accomplishments of their forebears. John Howard was not a denialist; he was defensive about his settler heritage. Of course, an inability to deal with the psychological meaning of this historical legacy often means the default position becomes a version of denialism – or is strongly coloured by denial. After all, the long, 150-year reign of the Great Australian Silence was about denial.

On the other hand, I observed that progressives were prone to use racial discrimination and historical denial as political bludgeons against their conservative opponents, and their advocacy for an honest confrontation with the colonial past degenerated into moral vanity. The result was that progressives reinforced victimhood of the indigenes while their opponents denied their victimisation.

Having said this, I now turn to the volatile question of the extirpation of the original Tasmanians.

I hoped to avoid the past, but it is not possible. I hoped to dis-remember the past, but it is not possible.

The question of genocide in Australia

The use of the term "genocide" and the rhetoric of the Jewish Holocaust is incendiary. The destruction of the Tasmanians was an event of world history long before the Nazi genocide of the Jews. It was well established in the discourse of British and Australian history long before the 1948 Genocide Convention. It was referred to around the world during the course of the nineteenth century and throughout the twentieth.

Whether you use the word most common in colonial times – "extirpation" – or other words also used – "extermination" or "extinction" – or the word "genocide," they speak to the same meaning. And that meaning is the loss to the world by the passing of a people from history by killing and mass death. The fact that a descendant community survived this history does not negate or reduce the profundity of the loss. When as a primary schooler I was told the significance of Truganini was that she was the last "full blood" of Tasmania, I understood clearly what was meant. The language of racial composition was commonplace in that time, and still is, among black and white Australians, despite its contemporary disreputability. It is not to deny the fact of the survival of the descendant community, and neither is it to impugn their identity, to remember the enormity of the fact that Truganini's death marked the passing from the world of one of the last Tasmanians without mixed lineage. A lineage that had occupied that land for more than 35,000 years.

Those last sentences were hard to write. I was not sure I could get it right, and still don't know whether I have. I mean not to offend contemporary Aborigines of Tasmania. I mean not to return to the mind-frame of racialist eugenics that has so tangled the history that I wish untangled.

I just do not want to deny or diminish the tragedy of Truganini and the old people of Tasmania.

Of course, as a reader of history and not a historian, I can hardly untangle this history. I can only say how I respond to and deal with it, as an Aboriginal and an Australian.

History is never resolved, and we should not make a shared future contingent on a shared past. For this reason I cannot abandon the examination of genocide as readily as some eminent historians in the wake of the History Wars prescribe.

I will not deal with the debate on whether the removal of children, identified by Michael Dodson and Sir Ronald Wilson in the *Bringing Them Home* report of 1997, constituted genocide. I will also not deal with the debate on whether the colonial history of mainland Australia – particularly my home state of Queensland – involved genocidal episodes. Instead I will confine my discussion to what happened in Tasmania in the first half of the nineteenth century.

Among historians who have been at the forefront of Aboriginal history, there is some respectable consensus against the use of the term "genocide" in this context.

Henry Reynolds' *An Indelible Stain?* centres on official correspondence from secretary of state for the colonies Sir George Murray to Tasmania's lieutenant governor, Sir George Arthur, on 5 November 1830. Murray referred to the "great decrease which has of late years taken place in the amount of the aboriginal population" and his apprehension "that the whole race of these people may, at no distant period, become extinct." He wrote:

> But with whatever feelings such an event may be looked forward to
> by those of the settlers who have been sufferers by the collisions
> which have taken place, it is impossible not to contemplate such a
> result of our occupation of the island as one very difficult to be rec-
> onciled with feelings of humanity, or even with principles of justice

and sound policy; and the adoption of any line of conduct, having for its avowed, or for its secret object, the extinction of the native race, could not fail to leave an indelible stain upon the character of the British government.

Reynolds' discussion focuses on the coining of the term "genocide" by the Polish Jewish jurist and American émigré Raphael Lemkin, in the 1940s, and its adoption in the Genocide Convention of 1948, following the Holocaust. Lemkin was clear that while the term and its establishment as a crime in international law was new, its occurrence in history was not. Lemkin specifically assumed that the events in Tasmania which I am discussing here constituted such an occurrence.

Applying the definition of the crime of genocide to events before the enactment of the Convention involves retrospectivity, and indeed its application to the Holocaust was necessarily retrospective. It was applied by Lemkin and is generally not considered anachronistic when applied to the history of the Armenians at the hands of Turkey in 1915. How far back does retrospectivity turn into anachronism?

But anachronism is not the only objection to taking terminology invented in the 1940s and applying it to events in colonial Tasmania. In his discussion in *An Indelible Stain?* and *Forgotten War* (2013), Reynolds comes down against the application of genocide to Australia because the 1948 Convention requires *intention* on the part of the offending state. The absence of an explicit intention on the part of the colonial authorities, who frequently expressed concern at the treatment of indigenous peoples at the frontier, ultimately underpins Reynolds' conclusion. It is a lawyer's conclusion. The lawyer in me protests that the circumstances and the evidence clearly speak of a constructive intention on the part of the colonial authorities, but this debate is not merely a legal argument. John Docker's point is apposite:

> We must also remember that in Lemkin's 1944 definition … the cultural and political were both strongly present as part of the manifold

ways the essential foundations of life of a group were being destroyed. Lemkin's 1944 definition and the Lemkin-influenced definition enshrined in the 1948 convention have acted in subsequent thinking about genocide like a double helix – neither reducible one to the other nor wholly separable. The definition of genocide, that is, always has a double character: both discursive and legal. In my view, we should not base the historical study of genocide on a legal definition alone; indeed, we should not base the historical study of any phenomena on a legal definition alone.

Inga Clendinnen, an authority on the Jewish Holocaust and respected Australian historian, also baulked at the application of the genocide definition to the Australian context:

> I am reasonably sophisticated in these modes of intellectual discussion, but when I see the word "genocide" I still see Gypsies and Jews being herded into trains, into pits, into ravines, and behind them the shadowy figures of Armenian women and children being marched into the desert by armed men. I see deliberate mass murder.

Bain Attwood's *Telling the Truth about Aboriginal History* (2005) was a fine circuit-breaker to the History Wars. He showed clearly that Keith Windschuttle's role in these debates was not as a historian. Windschuttle is a reader of history and public intellectual, not a historian, and *Fabrication* is a work of historiography, not history. I consider Attwood's book a good starting place for Australian readers of history to think about how we might come to terms with our past. I therefore take his view seriously:

> In my opinion, genocide is neither a necessary nor a useful concept for the task of understanding the nature of the white colonisation of this country.

But I remain unpersuaded that these views should be the final word. Let me enumerate my reasons.

First, the fact of Truganini.

Second, Michael Mansell's point that "the British had more impact on Aborigines than the Holocaust had on the Jews" is particularly apt in respect of the history of his people. The old people of Tasmania are no more. Only their descendants remain. (Lawson: "… if the destruction of their ancestors was not total, it was comprehensive. All original communities had been destroyed since the British invasion, and the population reduction was greater than 99 per cent.")

Third, I bridle at assessments that derogate from the gravity of what happened to the Tasmanians. In this respect I am resistant to Attwood's approach:

> in becoming the universal trope of trauma [the Holocaust] can also simultaneously enhance and hinder other historical and memorial practices and struggles. In the Australian context, it had undoubtedly done both. My concern here, though, is the way in which invoking the Holocaust has become, in some hands, a means by which other crimes are cast as minor by comparison to its absolute evil. As Peter Novick has argued, making the Nazi genocide the benchmark of atrocity and oppression can "trivialise" crimes of lesser magnitude. This is not merely a distasteful mode of speaking, but a truly disgusting one, he points out. Yet, as he suggests, it is one that readily occurs when something like the Holocaust becomes the touchstone in moral and political discourse.

Without in any way diminishing the Holocaust (as if it could be diminished), I cannot accept any moral comparison that diminishes the fate suffered by the Tasmanians.

Fourth, the accounts – both from the oral histories of Aborigines and from the documented sources of colonial times – referring to the death of Aborigines on the frontier speak to me of the profoundest moral problem of this history: the heavy discounting of the humanity of the Aborigines. It is not the horrific scenes of mass murder that are most appalling here;

it is the mundanity and casual parsimony of it all. No people on earth were considered lower. No people rated lower on the ruling scales of human worth, and their deaths elicited the least level of moral reproval. My point is that while the reproof of the time reflected the morality of the age, the racism that underpinned that calculus cannot hold sway today. The Tasmanians were human beings. They were gone within half a century. And only their descendants remained.

Fifth, there is Tom Lawson's thesis in *The Last Man*, to which I now turn.

The Scylla and Charybdis of colonialism

Tom Lawson is professor of history at Northumbria University in the United Kingdom. His book *The Last Man*, published this year, is subtitled *A British Genocide in Tasmania*. If his thesis has any power, it is to make plain that the consensus view outlined above is a long way from having resolved these questions. He puts forward a compelling counter-interpretation.

I will avoid a summation of Lawson's book, for it is better read in its own right. It is worth reading in its own right. Even if you come to these questions with scepticism or indeed indignation, you have a duty to hear out his scholarship.

If you read Lawson after Reynolds' *An Indelible Stain?*, you will be struck by a subtle but critical point made by the Briton about who would wear the indelible stain. For Reynolds:

> the question that Murray's words still confront us with is whether our history has left an indelible stain upon the character and reputation of *Australian* governments – colonial, State and federal – and upon the colonists themselves and their Australian-born descendants. [emphasis added by Lawson]

But in response, Lawson notes that:

> George Murray had not himself been that interested in the moral implications of genocide for the colony, but for the metropole. The

"indelible stain" that Murray feared was, it is worth repeating, upon the reputation of the British government.

It is a crucial reorientation of Reynolds' framing. The discussion of what happened to the Tasmanians in the first half of the nineteenth century is about a British colony run by the British government. The principal players in this history, Governor George Arthur, his predecessors and successors, his superiors back in Downing Street and their agents, such as George Augustus Robinson, on the colonial frontiers were members and agents of the British government, acting under the ultimate authority of the Colonial Office. They administered British policy, and this would remain the case until responsible government was vested in Tasmania in 1856.

It probably required a Briton to face this matter squarely. We might want to discuss the legacy bequeathed to subsequent pre- and post-Federation Australian governments and the colonists who were protagonists in and inheritors of this history, but Lawson's first point is that the destruction of the Tasmanians occurred in a British colony governed by the British Crown:

> This was a British genocide, carried out on the other side of the world by British men, articulating British ideas, discussed in British newspapers and ultimately embedded in British history and remembered in British museums.

This is Lawson's account of how an island population of several thousand was reduced to an official figure of seventeen inhabitants in fifty years:

> Some indigenous people in Tasmania died at the hands of settlers who wished to exterminate them. Some died in the process of being removed from land that settlers wished to develop. Some died in the process of being removed from the land and "civilised" into Europeans. Some died from warfare between the island's nations that was promoted by their declining resource bases, a

result of British presence. Some died of imported diseases. And, of course, some survived, but with little or no access to a culture that the British considered worthless and had attempted to destroy. This happened over the course of a colonisation played out during more than 50 years.

It is not Lawson's contention that there was a state project aimed at genocide – "clearly there was no state project of extermination in either Tasmania or continental Australia" – but rather that the colonial project itself had a fatal logic – "genocide was the inevitable outcome of a set of British policies, however apparently benign they appeared to their authors" – because "even those aimed at protection ... ultimately envisaged no future whatsoever for the original peoples of the island."

And this is the point that Lawson makes which is so compelling to me, and which is so important to grasp: indigenous Tasmanians were nearly extinguished between the Scylla of extermination and the Charybdis of protection.

These two pincers served the same ends: the preservation and continued prosecution of the colonial enterprise without relent, with sparing pity, but with no pause to the destruction it was so obviously causing the native peoples of the land being colonised, and of which the colonial authorities were acutely conscious long before the bitter end was reached.

This is how Lawson puts it:

> the British government knew explicitly that it had unleashed a destructive process that would eradicate those societies. Its representatives disavowed, and indeed even regretted, the exterminatory impacts of their presence, yet they never faltered, never sought to roll back colonial development. Indeed, they even developed an understanding of the world that saw as inevitable the dying out of "inferior" indigenous races.

Lawson's is a perspective-shifting analysis for me: that frontier destruction and protection served the same colonial logic. A logic that envisaged no future for the native peoples, whose homelands were to be usurped and societies swept aside by the expanding colonies. Which, in the case of the Tasmanians, led to utter destruction.

Of course, I have always understood that protection worked in concert with frontier dispossession, and facilitated it. It is just that protection seemed to be, if not pulling in an opposite direction, then at least divergent – ameliorating the harshness of frontier colonisation. Instead, protection pulled in the same direction as the frontier – which is what Lawson shows so powerfully in the case of its conception and inception in Tasmania.

I am a third-generation legatee of mission protection. The Lutheran mission at Cape Bedford started in 1886 was the initiative of Johann Flierl, a Bavarian missionary en route to German New Guinea. Waylaid in Cooktown, he started the mission after seeing the devastation of the Guugu Yimidhirr peoples in the wake of the Cooktown gold rush of 1873. The following year his successor, George Schwarz, took up Flierl's mission. The mission was an initiative of its society back at Neundettelsau, not of the colonial government of Queensland, but following the *Aboriginals Protection Act 1897* (later replaced by the *Aboriginals Preservation and Protection Act 1939*) the mission and the Queensland state became entwined. Pursuant to these laws, in 1910 my grandfather was removed from the bush as a boy. Dispossession on the frontier and the state's protection apparatus – native police "dispersing" the frontier tribes, protectors removing children to the missions, and Aboriginal reserves – led to what would be called the stolen generations. Protection provided new souls for the mission. What began in the 1880s as a safe haven for young women and an enticement for young men wanting partners, from 1900 turned into a receiving station for masses of huddled young, separated from their families.

Protection and preservation were not there for nothing. For the other side of Queensland's frontier had been and still was a charnel house: consisting of moments when the pitiless logic of colonialism ended in genocidal doom for some groups. As Queensland lacks the defining sea boundaries of the Vandemonian island, the annihilation of tribes on the frontier is more obscure. But there is a wide consensus in Aboriginal histories that the fiction of *terra nullius* was turned into the remorseless fact of *homo nullius* in some parts of Queensland.

As inheritors of the mission's religion and traditions, people like me necessarily hold complex perspectives on this history. The missionaries' kindnesses and humanity were mixed with the racialism of the time, and their objection to and support for various aspects of the colonial enterprise does not tell a simple story.

This dialectic has been part of my life and identity. The dingoes and sheep of my own exploration of our mission history as a student at Sydney University spoke to this historical and spiritual turmoil.

I will not get into the permutations of the protection regimes that emerged across the Australian mainland following George Augustus Robinson. The Tasmanian model was ameliorated with the setting aside of Aboriginal reserves in other states and the Northern Territory. The attitudes of the churches towards indigenous cultures, languages and heritage – and the conviction and vigour with which they sought to deracinate their charges – varied widely, according to the proclivities of particular denominations, individual missions within denominations, the personalities of key missionary figures, and the period of history. Therefore, while many missions and government settlements destroyed indigenous cultures and languages, others actively preserved them, and unofficially (and later sometimes officially) allowed Christianity to coexist with native religious beliefs. The language of the Guugu Yimidhirr survived because of Missionary Schwarz's conviction that their mother tongue best conveyed the Gospels to their hearts. Robinson's prototype house of confinement at Wybalena, Flinders Island, might have been the most extreme example, but its original logic remained at the core of all subsequent protection regimes.

So how is this to be dealt with? I cannot let Lawson's thesis on the Tasmanian genocide be set aside, and I also know that without the Lutherans my people would have perished on the Cooktown frontier. It is for me no longer an ambivalence; it is a clear understanding of the good and bad in the past. Yes, it is often said that history has many shades of grey, but this appreciation of complexity and nuance should not provide refuge from the truth that our nation's history includes times of unequivocal evil and times of redeeming goodness.

Whatever the ideological and symbolic villainy he represents to Aboriginal people, there is no mistaking Captain James Cook's extraordinary courage and stature as a seafaring explorer. Indeed, it is ridiculous to dispute it. For me, it is the same with Schwarz. I still cleave to my testimonial to the old man, published in *The Australian* on the eve of the parliamentary apology to the stolen generations:

> The nineteen-year-old Bavarian missionary who came to the year-old Lutheran mission at Cape Bedford in Cape York Peninsula in 1887, and who would spend more than fifty years of his life underwriting the future of the Guugu Yimidhirr people, cannot but be a hero to me and to my people. We owe an unrepayable debt to Georg Heinrich Schwarz and to the white people who supported my grandparents and countless others to rebuild their lives after they arrived at the mission as young children in 1910. My grandfather Ngulunhdhul came in from the local bush to the Aboriginal reserve that was created to facilitate the mission. My great-grandfather Arrimi would remain in the bush in the Cooktown district, constantly evading police attempts to incarcerate him at Palm Island and remaining in contact with his son Ngulunhdhul, and later his grandson, my father. My grandmother was torn away from her family near Chillagoe, to the west of Cairns, and she would lose her

own language and culture in favour of the local Guugu Yimidhirr language and culture of her new home. Indeed, it was the creation of reserves and the establishment of missions that enabled Aboriginal cultures and languages to survive throughout Cape York Peninsula. Today, those two young children who met at the mission have scores of descendants who owe their existence to their determination to survive in the teeth of hardship and loss. Schwarz embodied all of the strengths, weaknesses and contradictions that one would expect of a man who placed himself in the crucible of history. Would that we were judged by history in the way we might be tempted to judge Schwarz – we are not a bootlace on the courage and achievement of such people.

My childhood home was on the first street on the northernmost side of the village, named after Flierl. Next is the main street named Muni, a rendering of Schwarz's Guugu Yimidhirr name. These parallel streets name the key figures of our mission history in succession. The third is named after Wilhelm Poland, who, supporting Schwarz, raised a young family in the earliest years of the mission. A prolific writer and translator, he gave an account of the capture by troopers in July 1888 of Didegal, one of the Guugu Yimidhirr still living in the bush, who was suspected of killing a white man three months before. Didegal was treated as an outlaw, like my great-grandfather. Arrimi eluded police all his life, but Didegal did not:

> But, this time, Didegal's fate was sealed; he was the victim of his own treachery. On the following morning, his pursuers had little difficulty in tracing the clear imprint of his footsteps through soot and ash, and had completed their mission before midday. The man who was still planning mischief 24 hours previously now stood before us in irons, but with that characteristic look of sneering disdain still dominating his dark features. I must admit, I felt a certain compassion towards him. Was he not, after all, a poor, misguided heathen?

After a short break, the troopers saddled their horses, shouldered their guns, indicated to the captive that he was to follow them, and made their way back into the privacy and secrecy of the bush.

No one ever saw Didegal again. Some distance from the beaten track the party was ordered to a halt, a shot was fired, and Didegal was dispatched for good. He was, after all, only a black fellow.

This is what I mean by the casual parsimony of killing on the frontier. Anonymous, extrajudicial, unreported, mundane. Like eradicating vermin. Or inferior beings of human likeness.

LAYERED IDENTITIES

> [Australian] multiculturalism asserts that people with different roots can coexist, that they can learn to read the image-banks of others, that they can and should look across the frontiers of race, language, gender and age without prejudice or illusion, and learn to think against the background of a hybridized society. It proposes – modestly enough – that some of the most interesting things in history and culture happen at the interface between cultures. It wants to study border situations, not only because they are fascinating in themselves, but because understanding them may bring with it a little hope for the world.
>
> – Robert Hughes, *Culture of Complaint* (1993)

Bonding and bridging

In a 2006 essay I introduced the idea of layered identities as a way of understanding identity in pluralist societies. I thought the dominant metaphors of the "melting pot" and the "patchwork quilt" were too simplistic, the former implying some kind of muddy soup and the latter a diversity of patches held together in a united whole – but losing the idea that within each of these patches are layers of identity that extend beyond the patches, and sometimes across the whole quilt.

My thought was that by visualising identities as layers we would appreciate the richness and complexity of social identity. It enables us to see individuality and commonality. We can see what is common to members of groupings and what is individual to each member.

National identity is one layer – the largest and most significant within our country – but we can also identify as citizens of the world, or as members of the Anglosphere, the Jewish diaspora and so on. Although we are Australians, we are not just Australians: some of us are Queenslanders and others are South Australians. And we are not just Queenslanders: for some purposes, we are North Queenslanders or, more specifically still, Cape Yorkers.

And of course our identity as indigenous Australians is equally layered. At a continental level, we all think the black, red and yellow flag is a magnificent expression of our identity, but at a regional level we are also Kooris, Nyungars or Murris, and so on. At the traditional level, the layers are even more complex, comprising nations or tribes, language and dialect affiliations, clan and extended family estate groupings – encompassing songlines and common mythological tracks that traverse vast distances and involving numerous groupings.

At a linguistic level, there are commonalities that unite ancestral languages across Australia. The Guugu Yimidhirr I speak is part of a family of languages linguists call Pama-Nyungan (*pama* being the word for person in the languages of Cape York and *nyungan* being the word for person in the Nyungar languages of southwestern Australia). The ancient languages of the Pama-Nyungan family are spoken from Cape York down to the homelands of the Wiradjuri of New South Wales and across to Perth, and roughly from Mount Isa to Broome. Languages to the north and south of this largest grouping represent different families. This is why Guugu Yimidhirr from Cape York startle when they speak to Pitjantjatjara people from central Australia: the similarities between their languages are striking.

How people answer the question "What is your indigenous identity?" is therefore context-dependent. Whether people zoom in on their narrow clan affiliations or zoom out to a pan-Aboriginality depends upon the circumstances.

While ethnic and religious identities are primary layers, there are many other layers of shared identification: geography, historical association, recreational and social groups, intellectual and artistic communities, as well as sexual orientation and political and other modern cultural affiliations.

Some of these – such as sporting affiliations – may seem trivial compared to, say, ethnic identity, but actually they play important roles in creating connections across the more primary affiliations. These more ephemeral and seemingly unserious affiliations add to the great fund of capital in society which underpins social cohesion. That we may treat these affiliations with playful seriousness probably helps us to have a perspective that would be missing if we only had primary layers of identity. Sporting and other recreational codes and teams are not unimportant layers of identity.

My idea of layered identities complemented Amartya Sen's analysis in *Identity and Violence* (2006), where he referred to the "illusion of singular identity." Sen argued we should recognise "competing affiliations" and "competing identities," not in the sense of divided allegiances or a lack of loyalty to the sovereign state, but in recognition of the plurality of identities in any society.

Sen was particularly insightful in respect of multiculturalism. Although Australian conservatives have at times sought to criticise multiculturalism, the policy remains well regarded here. The electoral consequences of trying to abandon it, and the fact that leading liberals and conservatives are champions of its history, make their critique unlikely to prevail.

Yet Sen's analysis allows us to see what can be a problem with multiculturalism if you are concerned for national unity. When there is a singular focus on culture, as defined by ethnicity and religion, and a lack of emphasis on other layers of identity and affiliation, a problem can arise. Cultures become identity blocs when ethnicity and religion are seen as the single dominant affiliation.

Sen shows how opponents and supporters of multiculturalism often share the same illusion: the illusion of culture as a singular identity. There are therefore not just two possibilities – monoculturalism or multiculturalism – but a third as well: plural monoculturalism. This is when several singular identity blocs within a society are isolated and disconnected from each other. Having weak or no bonds with one another, these monocultures end up insular and resistant to a larger mutuality.

This is the potential weakness, not multiculturalism proper. Societies should guard against and work to prevent multiculturalism degenerating into plural monoculturalism, where groups end up raising cultural ramparts against each other.

An antidote to this is what Robert D. Putnam calls "social capital." In his *Bowling Alone* (2000), Putnam identified those things that contribute to bonding *within* religious, ethnic and socio-economic groups. But he also identified those things that contribute to bridging *between* groups, strengthening ties among disparate groups. His examples of such bridging include the civil rights movement and ecumenical religious organisations.

Plainly, Putnam's idea of social capital is directly applicable to an analysis of identity. Individuals and groups form bonding and bridging affiliations, and, as with the warp and weft of a multi-layered fabric, a society is all the stronger for them.

Fundamentalism and orthodoxy

Identity fundamentalism is the enemy of commonwealths. When individuals and groups elevate one layer of their identity to the exclusion of all others, then we have a problem. Such chauvinism can arise at the level of subgroups, and at the national level.

While fundamentalism is a problem, orthodoxy is not. Nations such as Australia have orthodox Christian, Jewish and Islamic communities without this being inconsistent with multicultural harmony. Political and cultural conservatives play the role of upholding the country's Anglo culture and inheritance. Like their non-Anglo counterparts, the conservatives of *Quadrant* and the Samuel Griffith Society are a minority, but they uphold traditions that serve society as a whole. Without a core of orthodox conservatives, modern societies would descend into a soulless cosmopolitanism. Conservatism respects memory, tradition, ritual and values that we have inherited, over and above an enthusiasm for the future and indulgence in the present.

T.S. Eliot's essay "Tradition and the Individual Talent" (1921) captures the vital presence of tradition in the contemporary productions of European artists:

He must be aware that the mind of Europe – the mind of his own country – a mind which he learns in time to be much more important than his own private mind – is a mind which changes, and that this change is a development which abandons nothing en route, which does not superannuate Shakespeare, or Homer, or the rock drawing of the Magdalenian draughtsman …

Someone said: "The dead writers are remote from us because we know so much more than they did." Precisely, and they are that which we know.

But orthodoxy that reduces to fundamentalism is not conservatism. True conservatism equips societies and peoples to contend with the modern world and change: it is not obscurant to the changing world. Conservatism understands that fundamentalism is antipathetic to the commonwealth.

Galarrwuy Yunupingu is an Australian conservative, and he desires to hold on to things older than Homer and the Bible. "Where would we be without Homer and the Old Testament?" Don Watson asked in a February 2014 essay in the *Monthly*. I think this is what Yunupingu means when he says of the song cycles of his culture: "My inner life is that of the Yolngu song cycles, the ceremonies, the knowledge, the law and the land. This is *yothu yindi*. Balance. Wholeness. Completeness." Yunupingu's question equivalent to Watson's is: where would my people be without the Yolngu song cycles? This question sits within a larger question: where would Aboriginal Australians be without the song cycles of Aboriginal Australia? And this question in turn sits within the largest question: where would Australia and Australians be without the song cycles of Aboriginal Australia?

At the 2014 Garma festival, I heard the renowned indigenous filmmaker and broadcaster Rachel Perkins give an arresting account of urgent work she is doing to record the remaining knowledge of songlines held by women in central Australia:

In Arrernte country, we were lucky to have a very big desert that kept the colonisers back for a further 100 years than the southern states.

Although we pride ourselves on holding onto elements of our classical culture – and although we have our language – the truth is, we are one generation from losing our songs.

These songlines connect us with other tribes – and most importantly connect us with each other in the Arrernte world.

She described how in 2013 she became aware of the desperate need for action:

The women were required to perform and open a festival in Alice Springs at Werlayte Thurre, the place of the Two Sisters Dreaming, where my father was born.

Gathered together to discuss the arrangements, we realised that the song for that place had been lost – an old lady had died, taking the song with her. Our neighbours, the Pitjantjatjara women, could teach us – as they knew the verses that connected their part of the songline with ours – but it was in their language, not ours. It wouldn't be appropriate, so it was unable to be performed. Of course people and culture innovate and we adapted.

However, this realisation galvanised us into action.

She went on:

We are working strategically, woman by woman, to create an inventory of our songlines, and then we intend to record and fully annotate them for future generations.

Yet we have identified perhaps only ten to twenty women, from the thousands of Arrernte women, who are still holders of these songs.

There is no funding for this type of project, so we dress it up as a documentary, or an online multi-platform project, when really what we want to do is record the songs, our dreamings, the first stories, the heritage that is the true and original Australian culture.

And then she laid out the big vision:

Our hope is that in 200 years a young Arrernte women, who may not have her language or her grandmother to teach her, will be able to listen and learn from these recordings made by her great-great-grandmother and sing the songs of her country: her birthright.

Our hope is that these songs will also be there for all Australians. So we can carry the ancient memory that binds us to this land we share.

Our hope is to create a model that might be used by other Aboriginal nations.

There is such great need for this work at this critical time to ensure the songlines continue to connect us all.

On this level, Perkins is a conservative in the sense that Yunupingu is. It is *one layer* of her cultural identity as an Arrernte woman. Her concerns, her valuation of what is important, her anxieties and energies are channelled into a conservative project: to keep the songlines of her people and Aboriginal people traversing the heart of the continent. Her sense of responsibility is that of a conservative.

But she is mostly known for another layer of her cultural identity: that of film-maker and artist. In this layer she is thoroughly modern, working at the boundaries of indigenous culture and the wider currents of global culture. Her politics are more leftist than not, making her more orthodox cultural concern even more striking for its obvious conservatism.

Perkins' layers of indigenous identity are complex and sui generis to her own choices and orientation.

The bicultural vision

Galarrwuy Yunupingu's brother Mandawuy probably did most to articulate biculturalism as the goal for the Aboriginal future in Australia. It was a vision which inspired me, and which we adopted in our thinking about the future of our children in Cape York Peninsula.

We see our future as living in two worlds and moving between each: the Aboriginal world and the wider world. These worlds are not just physical or geographical – though the homeland of the Aboriginal world provides its foundation. These worlds are a matter of mind-frame, and one can move between these two worlds in many contexts, not just physically. Just as the Orthodox Jew might be a lawyer or an entrepreneur during the week, but retreat for the Sabbath from sundown on Friday, Aboriginal biculturalism involves the ability to switch between layers of identity – from Mandawuy's participation in the ceremonial life of the Yolngu, to his leading a rock and roll band blending the modern forms of popular music and the language, dance and song of the Yolngu.

We should make two important observations about layered identities and the preservation of Australia's most ancient cultural heritage.

The first is that Aboriginal people desire a bicultural future and there is no monocultural past that we can return to. The Yunupingu brothers recognised this, and their life's work has been to show the viability and excitement of this vision – which they have done – and to secure the conditions for its realisation in the long-term – which they have not. Not yet.

The second is that, as Perkins said, the songlines of the women of central Australia are also the heritage of non-Aboriginal Australians. It is this culture that is the *Iliad* and *Odyssey* of Australia. It is these mythic stories that are Australia's Book of Genesis. For the shards of the classical culture of this continent to vanish would be a loss not only to its indigenous peoples but also to all Australians, and to the heritage of the world generally. We would all be the poorer for the loss.

It is in this sense that Australians all have a layer of their identity that connects them to the cultures, languages and lands of the continent. This is the true meaning of commonwealth.

LIBERTY IS RESPONSIBILITY: THE TORMENT
OF POWERLESSNESS

> To the older generations of Australians it seemed an impossible idea
> that there could be anything in the Aborigines or in their tradition
> to admire. The contempt has perhaps almost gone. In its place one
> finds, surprisingly widely, both interest and solicitude. But old con-
> tempt and new solicitude have a common element: a kind of sight-
> lessness towards the central problem of what it is to be black fellow
> in the here-and-now of Australian life. For this reason hundreds of
> natives have gone through, and will go through, the torment of
> powerlessness which Durmugam suffered.
>
>   – W.E.H. Stanner, "Durmugam: A Nangiomeri" (1959)

The democratic problem: our extreme minority status

The question of justice for Aboriginal and Torres Strait Islander peoples
within the Commonwealth of Australia concerns three features of our
condition.

The first is our putative membership of a *race*. This race was like no
other: at a time when the colonial world ranked races in a great chain, the
indigenes of Australia were considered the "lowest of the low." Today race
is freighted with this history, which casts a long shadow over contemporary Australia. I discuss later in this essay the need for us to be rid of race,
so I will not deal further with it here.

The second is that we are *indigenous* to this country. Andrew Bolt equates
indigeneity with race. It is a conflation that is made reflexively by many
Australians, but clearly wrong. All Australians – native and immigrant –
are indigenous to some place on the planet, and though the heritages of
many Australians are mixed and multiple, and may be obscured by history and genealogy, there is such a category as people who are indigenous
to a territory. Let us be plain: Galarrwuy Yunupingu is indigenous to *Terra
Australis*, and this is despite being of the same human race as Andrew Bolt.

The third is that we are a minority in the Australian commonwealth. Not just a minority, but an extreme minority: 3 per cent of the population. The extremity of our minority status is underlined when you compare the Maori in New Zealand with Aboriginal and Torres Strait Islander peoples in Australia. Each indigenous population is over 600,000, but Maori comprise 15 per cent of the New Zealand population. Though a minority, Maori are not an extreme minority in the way we are.

The numbers matter when they are this small, because it goes to whether the system of democracy enables an extreme minority to participate in a fair way. This is the discussion I now want to have.

Even absent the problems of race and racism, and the issues stemming from our indigeneity, there would still be the question of whether our extreme minority status means we are effectively shut out of the Australian democracy. Because ultimately the core of our democratic system – elected representation in parliaments – depends on numbers.

That indigenous Australians are spread throughout the country dissipates our electoral presence further, except in the one jurisdiction where there is a significant minority: the Northern Territory.

I want to focus on our extreme minority because I believe it is a defining feature of our condition. It is a crucial explanation of our predicament. If we were not so small a minority, we could participate in the Australian democracy and influence its institutions towards our aspirations. It would help combat the baggage of race and represent our indigeneity.

There are many ethnic minorities in Australia of equivalent or smaller size. Some of them face barriers of racism, but, I would argue, not to the degree that Aboriginal and Torres Strait Islander peoples do. And these minorities are not indigenous to the nation, with the particular colonial history that brought us to where we are. Indigenous people were displaced and dispossessed in the founding of British settlement and the development of the nation. Indigenous people therefore have a unique historical and legal relationship with the Australian government.

These three factors combined – the legacy of race, our indigenous identity and our extreme minority status – explain the nature of our predicament. It is a predicament of feeble democratic participation at best and exclusion at worst.

It explains why the Australian parliaments and executive governments simply do not work for Aboriginal and Torres Strait Islander peoples. Routinely and invariably. While Australians complain about politicians, governments and bureaucracies, our democratic institutions, systems and processes generally work for the majority. The electoral system ultimately drives responsive government. Not so for extreme minorities whose presence in that electoral system is negligible.

I think non-indigenous Australians get a wrong impression of the ability of indigenous people to get government to work for them. Australians think we hold our own, when the truth is quite different.

They think because of the tragedies besetting indigenous peoples and the egregious nature of our social and economic problems – reported in those mind-numbing and imagination-defying statistics – that we are in there defining and leading any societal response through government. But this is not the truth.

They think because of the prominent reporting of indigenous issues that this somehow reflects the power of indigenous participation. But this is not the truth.

They think because of the large budgetary appropriations in the name of indigenous affairs that this reflects a system that is working for indigenous Australians. But this is not the truth. The truth is there is a massive industry around these appropriations and it is predominantly non-indigenous.

They also think that because there are many prominent indigenous leaders, such as the late Charles Perkins, Lowitja O'Donoghue, the Dodsons, the Yunupingus, Marcia Langton and so on, this indicates a powerful political presence in the Australian democracy. This is not the truth.

The truth is this peculiar Australian system has produced more indigenous Australians of the Year (nine) than federal politicians (four). How is it that state and federal parliaments since 1967 are filled with successions of the most mediocre time-servers and yet they have never had a Patrick Dodson, Pat O'Shane or Warren Mundine?

The answer lies in our extreme minority status. The scale and moral urgency of the indigenous predicament far exceeds the power of indigenous participation in the country's democratic process.

We have to solve this democratic problem. It is the problem of the 3 per cent mouse and the 97 per cent elephant.

The historical problem: the question of consent

When James Cook first sailed the east coast of this continent on the *Endeavour*, he carried instructions contained in a letterbook dated 30 June 1768:

> You are also with the Consent of the Natives to take Possession of Convenient Situations in the Country in the Name of the King of Great Britain: Or: if you find the Country uninhabited take Possession for his Majesty by setting up Proper Marks and Inscriptions, as first discoverers and possessors.

History records that on 22 August 1770 Cook declared possession of the east coast of Australia. Cook noted the land was inhabited, but there was no documented negotiation with the natives. No deal was done, no formal friendship made, nor any alliance formed. Neither the land nor sovereignty over it was ceded by the Aboriginal peoples of *Terra Australis Incognita*.

There was no consent.

I set this out not to attempt anew some legal surgery on the scabrous wound of the country's legal foundations. The damage was done and the law of the colonists made the country's sovereign illegitimacy injusticiable (unable to be legally challenged in the courts). This truly was where might is right.

After the *Mabo* case, we now know that there were two aspects to the legal meaning of the sovereign settlement of Australia. The first is sovereignty, which the law refuses to deal with, saying it is injusticiable. The second is ownership of the land, which the law belatedly dealt with in

Mabo. The law posited native title: the beneficial ownership of land by the occupant native peoples, who were now subjects of the Crown and held their title pursuant to their customary laws, and whose possessions received the recognition and protection of the common law.

The lie of *terra nullius* was overturned in respect of the *legal* question of land ownership, but the *political* question of sovereignty could not be dealt with, let alone resolved.

I am not interested in tilting at the windmill of sovereignty as a question of *legal* legitimacy: this question has been put and will be put again by others more gallant than me. Instead, I am interested in discussing the *political* and *policy* implications of the absence of indigenous consent for the colonial claim to sovereignty. I will do this by looking at what played out in the absence of consent in this country – and the legacy with which we are grappling today – and considering how this played out during the Age of Empire in other parts of the world.

There is great variation in the histories of various colonies, but before I discuss these, I make the obvious point that *treaties* were the means by which the terms of any original agreement were captured between colonial powers and colonised peoples.

When a society seeks to take over the territorial sovereignty of another people, in the absence of war or seeking to avoid it, they *treat* with the pre-existing peoples. Treaties usually set out the terms early in the colonial story, sometimes after conflict but preferably in order to avoid it. Throughout history they were invariably dishonoured and conflict ensued, though their legacies in the present have not disappeared. These legacies are both legal and moral.

Then there are settlements that seek to address the failure to treat at the beginning of colonisation. Such settlements either revisit the dishonoured treaties of earlier times, or belatedly address those matters originally ignored.

I discern five permutations in how this has played out.

1   *No consent, independence movement, decolonisation*

Many colonies were established by colonial fiat, without the consent of existing peoples. Eventually there were independence movements and, following World War II, decolonisation. The European colonies in Africa and Asia fit this model. These were always cases where the native population far outnumbered the Europeans and independence was inevitable.

2   *Consent by treaty, dishonour, struggle, a new settlement*

This is what happened in New Zealand with the Treaty of Waitangi, and in North America. They were almost all dishonoured through colonial history. The native struggle has never abated, and in some cases led to new settlements. The revivification of the Treaty of Waitangi gave rise to what might be called a new settlement process in New Zealand, seeking to restore the honour of the Crown dishonoured through history.

3   *No consent, struggle, a new settlement*

This is what happened in South Africa, where the Europeans were a minority but powerful, and vigorously resisted the dismantlement of the apartheid that underpinned their power. There was a long and bitter struggle, and eventually a new democratic settlement that destroyed apartheid but did not vanquish the white minority – but included it.

4   *No consent, struggle, destruction / no accommodation*

This is what happened in Tasmania. As discussed earlier in this essay, the logic of colonisation made no accommodation for the original peoples of Tasmania – and policies of protection actually contributed to the destruction, rather than avoiding or ameliorating it.

5   *No consent, struggle, destruction / partial accommodation, no settlement*

This is where we are at in Australia today. There was no consent through an original treaty, and neither has there been a post-facto settlement. There have been partial measures of accommodation, but no settlement. The splinter in the mind of Galarrwuy Yunupingu is emblematic of the fact that these accommodations have not resolved the existential crisis of indigenous peoples.

To our north, closer to Cape York than Tasmania is to Melbourne, this same historical process is playing out in West Papua. I know not whether the situation is 4 or 5 in the above taxonomy. I hope it is 5, but fear it is closer to 4. I wonder what is really going on and how the West Papuans are faring between the Scylla of Indonesian sovereignty and the Charybdis of whatever accommodations have been made to protect them. In a world of instant communications we have fewer conversations about what is happening in West Papua today than took place in London during the colonisation of Van Diemen's Land in the early nineteenth century. And we Australians are well versed in blacking out a quadrant of our view.

Liberty, responsibility and self-determination

These three things are basically the same. There are differences according to provenance, but I think they coalesce around the idea of the freedom and power to choose. When liberals talk about liberty, when international law advocates talk about self-determination and when conservatives talk about responsibility, they are referring to the same phenomenon, albeit from their particular perspectives.

Liberty for the liberal is about individual freedom and the exercise of free will. The liberal believes in small government, wants to minimise the interference of government and law in the private domain of citizens, and wants to be certain that any interference is justified and authorised by the people through their democratic voice. The market liberal wants free trade with minimal government interference. But liberals understand that individual liberty has its limits: one must not harm others. The law must ensure the vulnerable are protected from abuse and unjust infringement of their liberty.

Further along the individual freedom spectrum, neo-liberals tend towards a free market with even fewer protections for the vulnerable. They are sceptical of any government interference aimed at remedying social injustice. They advocate a return to so-called "classical human rights." At its extreme, neo-liberalism, in its effort to resist social engineering, can become a penchant for unfettered survival of the fittest, with diminished regard for any sense of the social good. They deny the notion of "social justice." Individual freedom can become the only goal worth pursuing.

Liberty is at the heart of the current push for constitutional reform and recognition. The liberal and the neo-liberal, the classical liberal and the libertarian may well support constitutional reform to ensure all citizens are free and equal. This is because the purpose of a constitution is to limit and define the powers of government and to prevent arbitrary exercise of government power, so as to protect the liberty of citizens. By limiting and defining government power, individual freedom is implicitly protected. Individual liberty is therefore the core value all liberal democratic constitutions uphold.

Where the liberal talks freedom, the conservative believes individuals must take responsibility for themselves. Ultimately, though, the ideas are similar. Freedom entails responsibility. It is only with free choice that responsibility can be exercised.

Let me make one observation about the cherished liberal principle of choice. Choice is not just a freedom. Choice is a power, because with it comes responsibility. Once the individual makes her choice, she is obliged to wear the consequences: she must take responsibility for that choice – for good or for ill. She cannot blame others, or blame society. And if she has erred in her choice, it behoves her to remedy her error – not someone else. The popular conception of choice (among liberals and the libertarian left) as an unfettered and careless freedom overlooks that freedom of choice, properly understood, is in truth all about personal responsibility. This is the connection between the liberal principle of choice and the conservative principle of responsibility.

Indigenous Australians now want our equal liberty. We want the freedom to take responsibility.

Indigenous Australians have not prospered under Australia's Constitution, because our people were excluded from the liberty and equality established by that constitution for the benefit of all citizens. Section 25 demonstrates how we were excluded from democratic participation: we were prevented from voting and therefore from exercising our democratic rights. The Race Power, section 51(xxvi), allows the Commonwealth to pass special laws for so-called races in Australia, whether positive or adverse. It therefore empowers parliament to infringe our liberty on the arbitrary and unjust basis of race.

Australia's constitutional arrangements excluded indigenous people from the benefits of the liberty – and from the free and equal participation in democracy – that was, for other Australians, guaranteed. As a result, much discrimination was sanctioned. While the discrimination was explicit and malign at first, more recently we have seen a proliferation of well-intentioned positive discrimination – benign in intent, but still harmful to our individual liberty and thus to our personal responsibility. Such policies have too often entailed the "soft bigotry of low expectations" – perhaps the most felicitous phrase ever uttered by George W. Bush.

How can a liberal democratic constitution still allow race-based laws against its citizens? How can it still contemplate barring citizens from voting on account of race? The truth is the founding fathers abandoned liberal democratic principles with respect to race. It was an error reflecting the thinking of the time, but it needs to be rectified. For the suffering that indigenous people have experienced from this error is real. The loss of liberty meant the loss of personal responsibility. We were prevented from making our own choices. It meant real self-determination for our people could not be achieved.

Self-determination is a concept of international law, applying to nation-states and to individuals. It has also been the policy of the Australian government since the 1970s. But the problem, as Frank Brennan observed in 1993, is that here "the political term has no guaranteed legal content."

It has therefore been conflated with the lesser idea of self-management, whereby the indigenes are given management functions in policies that are determined by government. Brennan argued that a definite legal concept of self-determination for Aboriginal people should result from the logic of *Mabo*:

> An Indigenous community living within the nation-state and enjoying recognition of its legal system by the legal system of the nation is a community entitled to more than self-management. It is entitled to self-determination within the life of the nation.

The right to self-determination set out in the United Nations 2007 Declaration of the Rights of Indigenous Peoples is defined as the right of indigenous peoples to freely determine their political status and to freely pursue economic, social and cultural development.

Australia and New Zealand, like Canada and the United States, were hesitant in signing up to the Declaration, even though it was legally non-binding. Australia finally did so in 2009 and New Zealand in 2010, but not without reservations – the New Zealand government reassured its population that the Declaration would be implemented only insofar as it fitted in with New Zealand's legislative and constitutional arrangements. Australia is yet to implement any of the Declaration's clauses.

In reality, such declarations will always be non-binding on nation-states. Each nation must reach its own settlement and realisation of what the indigenous right to self-determination means within its own democratic institutions.

Indigenous self-determination is a domestic democratic question.

Our right to choose our future

If indigenous Australians desire a bicultural future, there are two roads we must walk down.

The first I call the Adam Smith road. This is the road of development and social and economic success in the modern, global world. This is a road we travel alongside other peoples of the world who are seeking to escape poverty and socio-economic deprivation. The rules of this road are culture-blind. They do not demand cultural assimilation, but they make equal demands on all cultures. There is no "culturally appropriate" version of Adam Smith's liberalism. Indians, Chinese, Jews and Ethiopians are not required to renounce their cultures, but the rules of liberal development rarely bend to these cultures: these cultures must instead accommodate the rules of liberal development.

This is not without its challenges for indigenous peoples, whose cultural traditions and institutions are often at odds with liberal development – communal land, kinship obligations, and so on – but these challenges are no different to those faced by cultures in earlier times. They made adjustments and accommodations between their culture and the imperatives of liberal development.

The second I call the Johann Herder road. The German philosopher (1744–1803) is as important for our cultural determination as Adam Smith is for our liberal development. I will discuss Herder later in this essay.

Bicultural people are not exactly rare. Europe and Asia are replete with examples of peoples who walk the Adam Smith road by day and the Johann Herder road by night. People who grow socially and economically strong without losing their languages and cultures.

These peoples have *integrated* but not *assimilated*. And they have chosen how they will adjust their culture to fit in with liberal development. They have not acquiesced to anyone's demand for deracination.

In Australia, indigenous peoples have not been allowed to make their own choices about how to reconcile their cultures with the demands of development.

One part of Australia urges the indigenes to renounce development in favour of preservation of some kind of imagined cultural purity. The environmental movement is particularly cynical in pushing this view, for its own ends. Its members prescribe a fictional approach to development for indigenous peoples which they themselves do not and could not ever live by. This is the adoption of the Noble Savage as the mascot for environmentalism.

The other part of Australia urges the indigenes to embrace development and to assimilate. This is the largest influence, and the default position of government policy, and it underpins the attitude of the average Australian. Indeed, the virulence with which commentators such as Gary Johns condemn indigenous culture indicates a depth of antipathy in Australia that is rooted in a troubled history.

Buffeted by these hectoring demands, indigenous peoples have not come to a clear understanding of how a bicultural future might be realised. Instead, they are pulled from one side to the other, and there is no national consensus that Aboriginal and Torres Strait Islander peoples desire a bicultural future where they are socially and economically developed and still maintain a strong culture. The next politician and the next bureaucrat coming around the corner has their own view on which of these priorities is more important – and on what should or should not be supported.

The only path to closing socio-economic gaps is for indigenous Australians to become active agents in our own development. Our poverty is a development problem that can only be solved by reversing our disenfranchisement. Calvin Helin asserts, "The responsibility for getting out of the welfare trap rests, first and foremost, squarely on the shoulders of indigenous people themselves." After all, indigenous people live the problems facing us. No one is better placed to solve the issues that confront us. Until indigenous Australians are allowed to take responsibility for our own lives, development and equality will not be achieved.

This is a fundamental shift. Indigenous policies to date have been premised upon exclusive and hierarchical conceptions of "race." They proceeded from historical assumptions of indigenous inferiority and incapability. These assumptions convinced governments that indigenous Australians are incapable, and, too often, they have convinced our own people.

We have now moved beyond the colonial assumption that the indigenous development predicament is a result of inadequacies innate to indigenous people or the darker-skinned "races." Such assumptions were condescending and untrue. They led to ineffective policies that still inhibit indigenous responsibility and empowerment.

Cultural recognition and equality are wholly compatible. Indeed, they are two sides of the same coin, tied together just as liberty is tied to responsibility.

The Japanese came to grips with the demands of Western development and capitalism in the middle of the nineteenth century, during the Meiji restoration. They made important decisions about how they were going to respond. They found a way of contending with the West while maintaining their ancient culture. Other nations and peoples have made similar accommodations.

British culture and traditions evolved as liberal capitalism developed. The Jews have made accommodations between their orthodoxy and their dealings with gentiles in the marketplace over a long period of time. Sometimes there was a steady social and cultural evolution, and sometimes conscious political and cultural realisation and decision.

But unlike other peoples who have contended with the challenge of development and cultural preservation, and unlike immigrants to Australia, indigenous Australians have been never been allowed to *determine their own* answer to this challenge.

Through discrimination we were denied access to liberty, and thus to development. Following this, the welfare era did not allow indigenous Australians to effect their own reconciliation between development and culture, because welfare is choice without consequence, choice without responsibility – and therefore not a real choice.

The choices that indigenous Australians might be said to have made ("I want to maintain my traditional cultures, but I still want to have all the vices of the Europeans"; "I want passive welfare to enable us to maintain our traditional lifestyles") are not real acts of self-determination.

Indigenous Australians must now take charge of our own development.

Otherwise, self-determination is the welfare version.

The virulent but sometimes subtle antipathy of some Australians to our existential claims is the source of the indigenous Australian anxiety. We need a constitutional imprimatur for the development formula and the cultural existence formula.

What does it mean to determine our own answer to the development challenge? It involves taking back creative control. Not just consenting.

There is something passive and hopeless in the word "consent." It makes it sound like we are lying down and saying yes or no to having things done to us, as though we are patients or lab rats consenting to medical procedures, or blushing virgins consenting to the controls and advances of some more knowing and masculine authority figure – a missionary, protector or latter-day Fat or Thin Controller of indigenous affairs.

Consent is something to fight for when it is all the law allows us. But consent is not the end-game. Ultimately, consent is too passive. We don't want to simply say yes or no to someone else's answers. We want to come up with the answers – yes, with the expertise and support and assistance of the best minds in the nation supporting us. Indigenous Australians, like any Australians, should have the right support and expertise. But no one knows the problem better than we do. We live the problem. No one is better placed to solve it.

Indigenous people need to think bigger than consent. We should instead talk about creative control. About coming up with solutions in equal partnership with government – or, better still, with indigenous peoples *leading the way* in indigenous affairs. Should not government consent to our policy and reform ideas?

The conservative understands responsibility. The liberal understands liberty. The indigenous activist talks of self-determination. They all ultimately speak of the same thing.

Now is the time for our people to be empowered: to take back liberty and responsibility.

We need the right constitutional "hook" for this to happen.

> We have to acknowledge that pre-1788 this land was as Aboriginal
> then as is it is Australian now and until we acknowledge that, we will
> be an incomplete nation and a torn people ... In short, we need to
> atone for the omissions and for the hardness of heart of our forbears
> to enable us all to embrace the future as a united people.
>
> — Tony Abbott, second reading of the *Aboriginal and*
> *Torres Strait Islander Peoples Recognition Bill*, 2013

The race error

Every nation is a unique creation. All democracies are not the same. Every
society that has ever created a constitution has had to deal with a unique
history and circumstances. There is no template democracy. There's no
template nation.

In 1901, when the Australian nation was created, it reflected the ideas
and biases of the time. One bias had as its cornerstone the exclusion of
the native peoples of this country. It took a long 66 years before that
exclusion from citizenship was remedied in 1967. Back when the referendum was crafted and overwhelmingly endorsed by the Australian
people – 90 per cent of the country voted in favour of it – there was not
one indigenous lawyer in the country, let alone an indigenous constitutional lawyer involved in the drafting of the amendment. Now, leading
indigenous legal intellectuals such as Professor Megan Davis are driving
these developments.

Even the greatest democracies are a search for a better unity. National
democracy is not just a lapidary achievement. No nation has created the
perfect unity. Facing racial conflict, President Barack Obama invoked the
idea that the United States is on a journey to a "more perfect union."
Ours is a journey to perfect our commonwealth and the unity it is
intended to represent.

During my involvement on the Expert Panel on Constitutional Recognition of Aboriginal and Torres Strait Islander Peoples, set up by Julia Gillard, I became convinced that the basis of our inclusion in Australian citizenship in 1967 was fatefully wrong. We were included as citizens of our own country on the basis of race, and that too reflected the bias of the time. In the decades leading up to the 1950s and 1960s, and for a long time after, it was commonplace to talk about people of different races. So it is understandable that in 1967 the basis of our citizenship was determined in section 51(xxvi) – the race clause. In retrospect, I saw – largely through the arguments of my colleagues on the panel – that our inclusion in the citizenship of the country on the basis of our alleged race was a momentous misstep.

It was wrong in fact. Today we understand that there are no races. And as long as human societies have assumed and perpetuated the idea that there are distinct races across the world, much misery has resulted. Today we understand there are no distinctions to be made among peoples on the basis of race. We are a human race. While we do not share a uniform culture, language, religion and ethnicity, we do share one characteristic: we are members of a single race.

As long as we have a constitution that characterises Aboriginal and Torres Strait Islander peoples on the basis of race, it will have deleterious implications for their citizenship. It must be removed. With the knowledge of hindsight, we must perfect the basis of our inclusion in the nation.

I believe the psychological and practical implications of these reforms will be profound. This is not just a matter of symbolism. I think this will be a matter of psychology. The day we come to regard ourselves as people with a distinct heritage, with distinct cultures and languages but not of a distinct race will be a day of psychological liberation. And it will also be liberating for those in the wider community who treat us as members of a distinct race, with all of the freight that accompanies this.

I believe constitutional reforms that remove the concept of race will have concrete, practical implications for indigenous wellbeing across this country. We have made many gains since 1967, but we have been significantly hobbled as well. And the chief thing that has hobbled us is the concept of race. This does not mean that when we get rid of race in our thinking, racism will not exist. There will still be discrimination. But such discrimination is based on an illegitimate idea: that people are different according to some racial criterion. So there will be need for protection against the illegitimate concept through the *Racial Discrimination Act 1975*. I see no contradiction in banishing notions of race from our constitution while at the same time ensuring protection of peoples against the illegitimate use of this distinction.

Our nation in three parts

On 15 July this year I had the honour of joining Rupert Murdoch and Tony Abbott in Sydney at the fiftieth anniversary of the founding of *The Australian* newspaper. In my remarks I said that:

> When the history of indigenous reform is written, the place of *The Australian* under the editorship of Chris Mitchell will be plain ... Mitchell opened the pages of *The Australian* to all shades of debate and indigenous leaders and commentators: no other mainstream platform comes close. Like the paper's founder, the paper's editor these past 12 years seems impelled by an unremitting sense of native duty to the nation by taking his indigenous brethren with utmost seriousness. Rosemary Neill's courageous coverage of tragic violence against Aboriginal women. Tony Koch's pursuit of Mulrunji's death at the Palm Island watch-house. Paul Toohey's searing stories of the petrol-sniffing Hades in the centre. These all echo the proprietor's campaign in *The Advertiser* in the Max Stuart case in 1959 abolishing the death penalty.
>
> *The Australian* treated these subjects not because it believed the country's indigenous peoples innocent or guilty, right or wrong, noble or ignoble – but because the paper believed in our humanity,

and that we and our affairs should not be left on the woodheap of the democracy. No paper welcomed indigenous writers and political leaders more than this one. The late Charlie Perkins, Marcia Langton, Galarrwuy Yunupingu, Patrick Dodson, Lowitja O'Donoghue, Warren Mundine and more have been regular protagonists in the national conversation in the national paper.

For those like me whose reform policies have been steadfastly supported by the paper's editorials, we have not been spared contrary views and criticism in news reporting and commentary. The dialectic of the national conversation plays out in the pages of *The Australian*.

This was a privilege for me: to witness Rupert Murdoch, one of those rare Australians whom the thoughtful senator from Queensland Brett Mason – in a forthcoming book on such figures – correctly identifies as having in some way *changed the world*, pause to reflect on a 50-year milestone on his journey. I think that not to marvel at Murdoch's colossal media exploits and take some borrowed pride from the fact that, like Don Bradman in cricket or Howard Florey in medical science, he is Australian is as absurd as denying the global impact of Robert Hughes on art or Germaine Greer on feminism. There may or may not be some validity in the suggestion that the levelling instinct of Australians is a salient contribution of indigenous peoples to the national character, but at the heart of that instinct lies a cringe that makes us a smaller nation, with a smaller sense of our own possibilities, when we don't recognise it as a double-edged sword. I suspect our aggressive egalitarianism is the engine that drives individuals to take on the forces of the establishment – witness the Dirty Digger taking over the London *Sun* – but it can also see the rest frantically determined to chop down the very outliers who have challenged and beaten the powers-that-be. This is our psychological, rather than cultural, cringe. One side of our egalitarianism challenges the status quo and the other preserves it through levelling.

It was for me a signal event. I tell this story to give a context to my final remarks to that audience, in which I set out how constitutional recognition of indigenous Australians would allow the nation to reveal our true nature and the great hidden architecture of our Commonwealth:

> Our nation is in three parts. There is our ancient heritage, written in the continent and the original culture painted on its land and seascapes. There is its British inheritance, the structures of government and society transported from the United Kingdom fixing its foundations in the ancient soil. There is its multicultural achievement: a triumph of immigration that brought together the gifts of peoples and cultures from all over the globe – forming one indissoluble commonwealth.
>
> We stand on the cusp of bringing these three parts of our national story together – our ancient heritage, our British inheritance and our multicultural triumph – with constitutional recognition of indigenous Australians. This reconciliation will make a more complete commonwealth.

The colonial history which I have revisited in this essay is the reason why the relationship between our indigenous heritage and the country's British heritage has eluded us. As troubled as this history is, and as troubling as it will be for the foreseeable future, these two things are the heritage of Australia. There is no denying it. It is the reality and it is the truth, no matter how much white Australians might want to ignore it or black Australians might want to reject it. Whatever the mutual denial of the past, the future must be one of mutual recognition.

> [Edmund] Burke developed three ideas that, it seems to me, were then and ought to be now the core of conservative thinking: respect for the dead, the "little platoon" and the voice of tradition ...
>
> Burke was one of the first major political thinkers to place future generations at the heart of politics ... Burke's view of society, as an association of the dead, the living and the unborn, carries a precious hint as to how the responsibility for future generations arises. It arises from love, and love directed towards what is unknown must arise from what is known. The future is not known, nor are the people who will inhabit it. But the past is known, and the dead, our dead, are still the objects of love and veneration. It is by expending on them some part of our care, Burke believed, that we care also for the unborn. For we plant in our hearts the transgenerational view of society that is the best guarantee that we will moderate our present appetites in the interests of those who are yet to be.
>
> — Roger Scruton, *Green Philosophy* (2012)

Love of home

"Love of home" – oikophilia – is the intriguing idea put forward by the English philosopher Roger Scruton in *Green Philosophy: How to Think Seriously About the Planet*. It is, I think, a most important contribution to how the pressing environmental problems facing human societies might be thought about and responded to. Scruton's book brings together the conservation latent in political conservatism and the conservatism latent in environmental conservation – love of the *oikos*, or household, is the common motivation in stewardship and protection of environment and society.

This common motive is for Scruton natural: the shared love of place:

> That, it seems to me, is the goal towards which serious environmentalism and serious conservatism both point – namely, home,

the place where we are and that we share, the place that defines us, that we hold in trust for our descendants, and that we don't want to spoil.

... it is time to take a more open-minded and imaginative vision of what conservatism and environmentalism have to offer each other. For nobody seems to have identified a motive more likely to serve the environmental cause than this one, of the shared love for our home. It is a motive in ordinary people. It can provide a foundation both for a conservative approach to institutions and a conservationist approach to the land. It is a motive that might permit us to reconcile the demand for democratic participation with the respect for future generations and the duty of trusteeship. It is, in my view, the only serious resource that we have, in our fight to maintain local order in the face of globally stimulated decay.

Environmentalists staring at the stark and impenetrable wall of liberal self-interest frustrating their schemes to turn around environmental decay should read Scruton and pause to reflect on where the mobilising of imposed large-scale bureaucratic strategies against the self-interest of *homo economicus* has ended up. Put aside your fantasies of eco-revolution and the great green uber-internationale – Scruton proposes another motive potentially as compelling as self-interest: the natural love of home.

Oikophilia is the closest that contemporary conservative philosophy comes to the indigenous love of homeland, but Scruton contrasts religious and kinship affiliations with national ones. Incorrectly, in my view, he makes assertions about tribal affiliations, which must be answered if his notion of oikophilia is to find common ground with the indigenous connection to country. This is the difficulty:

It is in contrast with tribal and religious forms of membership that the nation should be understood. By a nation I mean a people settled in a certain territory, who share language, institutions, customs and a sense of history and who regard themselves as equally committed both to their place of residence and to the legal and political process that governs it. Members of tribes see each other as a family; members of religious communities see each other as the faithful; members of nations see each other as neighbours. All these forms of self-identity are rooted in belonging and attachment. But only the sense of nationhood makes territory central and, in doing so, provides the first-person plural adapted to the society of strangers, and to the peaceful coexistence of people who share no family loyalties or religious creed. First and foremost the nation is a common territory, in which we are all settled, and to which we are all entitled as our home ...

To put the matter simply: nations are defined not by kinship or religion but by a homeland.

Of course homelands are central to tribes. Scruton's knowledge of the nature of tribal societies and their relationship with territory is too thin, and this is not his main concern, in any case. That is a pity. Because he would realise that his concept of tribal institutions ("The idea of an impartial rule of law, sustained in being by the very government that it sustains, has no place in the world of kinship ties") is limited. After all, it was in respect of Galarrwuy Yunupingu's Yolngu society that Chief Justice Blackburn famously observed in 1971 that:

> The evidence shows a subtle and elaborate system highly adapted to the country in which the people led their lives, which provided a stable order of society and was remarkably free from the vagaries of personal whim or influence. If ever a system could be called "a government of laws, and not of men", it is that shown in the evidence before me.

Scruton would recognise his description of the filial relationship between the Englishman and his native nation resonates with that between the Yolngu and his tribal nation – and speaks to the same conservatism.

The barrier that stands in the way of this recognition is Scruton's point about the exclusivity of the tribe: "when it comes to outsiders – the 'strangers and sojourners' in the land of the tribe – they are regarded as outside the law altogether and not entitled to its protection" and "Nor can outsiders easily become insiders, since that which divides them from the tribe is an incurable genetic fault."

Scruton's objections can be overcome if we accept layered identities. In this way the universal filiation is national citizenship with one rule of law and system of government. The one rule of law and system of government that applies in Scruton's native Britain is one which does not oblige – and in fact *cannot* oblige – unfreedom of religion. In the same way that this one rule of law and system of government preserves and upholds all manner of arcane institutions of inherited privilege (staunchly defended by conservatives from Burke to Scruton), so too are tribal nations consistent with the idea of the commonwealth.

The problem with Scruton's view of the tribe is that it is a dated caricature. It might have been true at the time of David Livingstone's adventures in Africa, the Australians making first contact in the highlands of Papua New Guinea or the first whites entering Arnhem Land, but it is now a view of the past. No tribes today live in isolation from other societies: they live within nations, where layers of history have left layers of identity. These tribes cannot be expected to abandon the institutions of their inheritance, inextricably bound as they are to the homelands of their inheritance. It would be as indefensible as expecting the inheritors of Britain's ancient entitlements to forsake their inheritance.

I want to now discuss one aspect of Scruton's idea of conservatism – respect for and connection with the dead – as part of a consideration of what it means to be indigenous.

In this passage from the International Court of Justice's 1975 *Western Sahara* case, Judge Ammoun captured what lies at the core of the idea of peoples being indigenous to a territory:

Mr Bayona-Ba-Meya goes on to dismiss the materialistic concept of terra nullius, which led to this dismemberment of Africa following the Berlin Conference of 1885. Mr Bayona-Ba-Meya substitutes for this a spiritual notion: the ancestral tie between the land, or "mother nature", and the man who was born therefrom, remains attached thereto, and must one day return thither to be united with his ancestors. This link is the basis of ownership of the soil, or better, of sovereignty.

I am not now concerned with the legal question. I am concerned with the metaphysical question: the *spiritual notion*. The ancestral tie between the land and the man who was born therefrom. Who remains attached thereto. And who must one day return thither to be united with his ancestors.

This is it. This is the nub. This is the essence. This is the source.

Before we have the abstraction of law, we have things that are real. The law is not the origin. It is the ancestral bones in the land that is the source. It is the dust of the ancestors mixed with the dust of the land.

It is from that land and dust that the people of the present came. And it is to that same dust and land that they remain attached. And it is to the same land they will "one day return ... to be united with [their] ancestors."

At the core of all Aboriginal customary law you find these elements. The ancestral tie to the land, the person born from that land, who remains attached to the land and whose spirits will one day return to that land. I would venture to say that these ideas are universal to all indigenous conceptions of relationship to their country, the world over.

My point is that it is not the law that is the wellspring of indigeneity: it is a reality concerning the dead, the living and the people to come, and the country to which they are tied. It is a similar reality of which Scruton writes when he refers to "Burke's view of society, as an association of the dead, the living and the unborn." If Burke's association is real, then it is real in the sense captured in Judge Ammoun's most apposite definition.

On this interpretation it is theoretically possible to take Andrew Bolt seriously when he protests that he too is indigenous to this country. The bones and dust of his ancestors and all settler and immigrant Australians who made this continent their home have been accumulating and mixing with the ancient soil for 226 years. Aboriginal laws and customs recognise the connections that arise from places of birth and burial. In a real sense the Bolts are becoming indigenous to Australia. Perhaps he could recognise in turn that the bones of Galarrwuy Yunupingu's ancestors have been returning for millennia to the lands from which they arose.

Man cannot live by bread alone

The Cape York agenda I have championed has elements of all three great traditions of political philosophy. This is how I explained it in *Up from the Mission*:

> The metaphor of the staircase may provide some fresh insight into why our agenda has so often proven to be so difficult to categorise in conventional political terms. Our focus on social norms has an inherently conservative flavour. But we also emphasised the critical importance of supporting capabilities – and this has a distinctly social-democratic flavour. Then we talk about incentives, the steps that allow people to choose to build their own lives; this has a distinctly liberal flavour.

I now see that while the liberal component of our agenda is well developed, the conservative element is not.

It is still a caricature of conservatism. Conservatism is not just about social norms. It is the insight that human beings will not be content when the liberal and social-democratic agendas are fulfilled.

If the engine of self-interest is cranked up, if the structure of incentives is right, if people exercise choice, if private property is well developed, if there is social-democratic provisioning of opportunity and people take responsibility to seize opportunity to build their capabilities – then what people will really want to do is to read the Talmud in Hebrew and Aramaic, or learn archaic Guugu Yimidhirr from old recordings, or build a scale model of King Solomon's temple.

Aboriginal Australian culture is evidence that when humans are at equilibrium, people build traditions tied to language and land and pass them on to the next generation.

Conservatism is not sending your children to school to paint your fence white. It is insight into the imperfection and mystery of human nature. This imperfection and mystery will ultimately make liberal and social-democratic structures inadequate and *binhdhu*, without taste.

Conservatism is the idea that distinct peoples should continue to exist because difference is an end in itself. The homogenisation inherent in liberalism and social democracy is risky because it robs us of many attempts to answer the great existential enigmas.

Conservatism is qualitatively different to liberalism and social democracy. Liberalism is based on a few principles, and then people do the rest through their own choices. But there is no end to the number of human traditions. Japanese and Guugu Yimidhirr liberalism are the same; Japanese and Yolngu social democracy are similar; but Japanese and Guugu Yimidhirr and Yolngu traditions are different worlds.

Tradition is by definition about the detail and not the broad principle. To work politically for tradition, you have to make sure the dictionary in ten volumes is written, for example. You have to record and teach the songs that traverse the continent.

Self-interest is the engine that drives everything else in the vehicle of progress. But tradition is the engine that drives human existence.

Johann Gottfried Herder thought Emperor Joseph II was wrong to enforce one official language in his empire. Herder's *Letters for the Advancement of Mankind* (1791) contains a fictional dialogue called "Conversation after the Death of Emperor Joseph II".

A. Which innocent preconceptions of the people did the Emperor Joseph offend?

B. Of many I mention but a few; first the preconception of language. Has a people, especially an uncultivated people, anything more dear than the language of their fathers? In it lives its entire wealth of thoughts about tradition, history, religion and principles of life, all its heart and soul. To take from such a people their language or debase it amounts to taking from them their only immortal property, which passes from parents to children.

A. And yet Joseph knew many of these peoples personally and very well.

B. The more it is to be amazed at, that he did not discern the intrusion. "Who suppresses my language for me," thinks the simple man not without reason, "will also rob me of my ability to reason and my way of life, my honour and the laws and rights of my people." Obviously, as God tolerates all the world's languages, so should also a ruler not only tolerate the different languages of his subject peoples, but also honour them.

A. But he wanted to achieve a more expeditious prosecution of commerce, a faster moving culture.

B. A people's best culture is not fast; it does not allow itself to be forced through a foreign language. It thrives at its most beautiful and, I would like to say, exclusively on the nation's own land in its inherited tongue. With the language one captures the heart of the people, and is it not a grand idea to plant the seed of well-being in the most distant future among so many peoples, Hungarians, Slavs, Romanians, completely in line with their own way of thinking, in their most distinctive and loved fashion?

A. It appeared to him to be a grander idea to amalgamate if possible all his states and provinces to one code of laws, to one education system, to one monarchy.

B. A favourite idea of our century! But is it feasible? Is it reasonable
   and beneficial?

Conservatism makes the case for continued existence in a deep sense –
not just in the trivial sense of having biological descendants.

Continued existence is of lesser concern to Anglophone (or Sinophone)
conservatives, because their cultures are too large and powerful to die.
Theodore Dalrymple may think people should read more books, but he
has no existential angst that there will be no one left who can and will
want to read Shakespeare.

Man needs bread, but he cannot live by bread alone.

Conservative arguments for constitutional reform

There are two reasons Australian conservatives should support constitutional recognition of Aboriginal and Torres Strait Islander peoples. First,
conservatism sees intrinsic value in tradition and inheritance – like our
British heritage, indigenous tradition and inheritance is important and
should be recognised and maintained. Second, conservatives value
national unity. They disavow separatism, collectivism and division among
citizens, preferring instead individualism bound by a common sense of
national unity and patriotism. That is why they should support the
removal of references to "race" that serve to divide citizens.

In trying to understand conservative objections to the Expert Panel's
proposals, it is important to understand the Australian mix of liberalism
and conservatism, and the influence of constitutional conservatism – the
influential group of Australian constitutional experts whom Greg Craven
dubbed the "con-cons." This group, convening as the Samuel Griffith
Society, values liberalism and democracy. They insist on parliamentary
sovereignty and are ready to accuse judges of usurping parliamentary
democracy. They value the Australian Constitution as inherited wisdom.

It is because, as Waleed Aly observed in Quarterly Essay 37, "tradition
has its own force and wisdom" that the conservative disposition prefers

organic evolution to revolution in society. Conservatives approach constitutional reform with extreme caution. According to Aly, conservatism is "resistant to ideological zeal": it "eschews utopian designs and adopts far more modest and pragmatic approaches to policy."

This explains conservative resistance to including principles such as "equality" or "non-discrimination" in the constitution. While valuing free and equal participation in a liberal democracy, conservative pragmatists do not think such ideals can be protected simply by writing them into the constitution. Such alterations risk giving the judiciary too much power.

In their strong aversion to activist judges, constitutional conservatives tend to forget the history that has driven this conversation about constitutional recognition.

Conservatives are concerned with limiting judicial activism, and therefore do not want symbolic words or sweeping "rights" clauses in the constitution. Indigenous advocates need to take these views on board. But what conservatives in turn need to understand, in an effort to find consensus, is that for indigenous people the movement for constitutional recognition has always been about achieving *constitutional protection and recognition of indigenous rights and interests within Australia*. It is about reconciling the fact that there were *peoples* here before the British arrived, and making provision for those peoples and their interests to be recognised within the nation. Symbolism and poetry is only one part of it. *Substantive change in the national approach to indigenous affairs* is the other.

Conservatives need to understand our position too. Our people lived through the discrimination of the past. We have a legitimate anxiety that the past not be repeated, and that measures be put in place to ensure *things are done in a better way*. If conservatives assert that a racial non-discrimination clause is not the answer, then what is a better solution?

In a recent paper, "The Australian Declaration of Recognition," Julian Leeser and Damien Freeman assert that the constitution is a rulebook, a practical charter of government that sets out power relationships, such as between the Commonwealth and the states. It is not a vehicle for aspirations and symbolism: these can be articulated in a declaration, not in the constitution proper. But if the constitution is a practical rulebook governing national power relationships, then we should also accept that there is one very important national power relationship that it clearly does not address. Arguably, therefore, the rulebook should be amended to make provision for indigenous people to be heard in indigenous affairs.

After all, if unelected judges should not decide what is in the interests of indigenous people, then who should decide? Indigenous people comprise only 3 per cent of the population, and hardly get a fair say in parliament, even on matters directly concerning them. Parliaments have never been good at listening to indigenous people. This is why the discrimination of the past has occurred. This is the elephant and the mouse problem that has characterised indigenous affairs.

We can find a way of ensuring that indigenous people get a fair say in laws and policies made *about us* without compromising the supremacy of parliament. Perhaps we could consider creating a mechanism to ensure that Indigenous people can take more responsibility for our own lives *within the democratic institutions already established*, and without handing power to judges.

As mentioned, conservatives should agree with the removal of racial discrimination from the constitution. They believe in national unity and dislike internal divisions, separatism and collectivism. They must now also turn their minds to how the constitution might be altered so that the discrimination of the past cannot happen again. We don't want separatism: we want inclusion on a fair basis. We want to be inside the decision-making tent. We want our voices to be heard in political decisions made about us. A mechanism like this – guaranteeing the indigenous voice in indigenous affairs – could be a more democratic solution to the racial discrimination problem.

Constitutional recognition could therefore include removal of the race clauses and the insertion of a replacement power to enable the Commonwealth parliament to pass necessary laws with respect to indigenous peoples, and incorporation of a requirement that indigenous peoples get a fair say in laws and policies made about us. A new body could be established to effect this purpose, and to ensure that indigenous peoples have a voice in their own affairs.

An agenda for the classical culture of ancient Australia

Distinct peoples the world over hold hard to four things: their identity as a people, their territories, their cultural heritage and their language. These lie at the core of what is indigenous about those Australian citizens who are Aborigines and Torres Strait Islanders. Let us look at how they have been accommodated in Australia.

The indigenous identity of Aboriginal and Torres Strait Islander peoples is recognised at a certain level. The Aboriginal and Torres Strait Islander flags are recognised as official flags under the Flags Act 1953. They fly outside parliaments, schools, council chambers and other public buildings. They are found on lapel pins of leading politicians and have become an accepted part of the public symbolism of the country.

But below that there is no official recognition of the many tribal nations associated with particular territories. Apart from the registrations that occur under land rights schemes, there is no official status or recognition accorded to first peoples. Some towns and cities have signage at airports or at the entrance of towns, or at public buildings which acknowledge local tribes – but it is not part of any official scheme of recognition.

"Welcome to country" ceremonies and the practices of acknowledging traditional custodians are now part of official protocols in Australia, even if there is more psychological discomfort about it than in, say, New Zealand – where the practice is de rigueur, sincere and there is no question of embarrassment. I witness many Australian ceremonies that are perfunctory or awkward, reflecting the degree to which we are far from the bicultural society New Zealand has become.

No doubt it helps if you have the greatest team of any sporting code in the modern world – the All Blacks – but it is impossible not to feel comparatively impoverished when the haka is performed and "God

Defend New Zealand" is sung in Maori and English. I am afraid to say one wipes tears for the hymn of our enemies and cringes at our own.

The other area of great work that lies before us is the naming of places throughout the continent. Thousands of cities, towns, suburbs, streets, bridges, rivers, creeks and other landmarks have Aboriginal names accumulated over two centuries. By the time you count all of the private names of homesteads, farms, residences, buildings and institutions that are Aboriginal, they number in the tens of thousands.

And yet there is little awareness of the provenance of these placenames. People seem not to know that Coolum is an Aboriginal name, as are the great majority of the town names on the Sunshine Coast. It is strange indeed to drive through places with virtually no Aboriginal presence, but all bearing these ancient names. Many Australians simply do not know the difference between Aboriginal and English names. My children and I play a kind of Gregory's street-map game of ancient Australia – where we get points for finding Aboriginal names: Cooroy, Noosa, Tinbeerwah, Eumundi, Beerwah, Maroochydore, Nambour. And then we pass the roundabout and see this sign: Murdering Creek Road. And I fall silent.

I will make a wild guess and say that fewer than one in a hundred of the ancient names of Australia have been officially recognised. Most features of the continent, its contours, swamps, sandhills, creeks, rivers, headlands and so on, have Aboriginal names of ancient provenance. How can it be that these names are not officially recognised? Other countries have adopted dual naming practices.

When I visit Yuurrgubarraalbigu, on the coast near the old Cape Bedford Mission, I pass a hill with the prosaic but official name of Round Hill, but its true name is Dhamal Nubuun: One Foot. It is ridiculous that a place that had a name at the time of Jesus of Nazareth is no longer officially known by this name.

This is a vitally important agenda for the country. This continent is a named continent, and Australians should know this landscape is rich with meaning and history.

Through land rights schemes, native title rights at common law and under legislation, land reservations and purchases, much has been done to recognise the territorial rights of the contemporary descendants of the original Aboriginal and Torres Strait Islander tribes. This is where accommodation has been made, and the process is by no means complete.

The protection of indigenous heritage in the form of cultural artefacts and places has long been provided for in legislation. These are of mixed quality and there are gaps, but this is an area of accommodation that has received attention.

There are institutions for keeping and displaying the country's indigenous heritage, including a dedicated institution – the Australian Institute of Aboriginal and Torres Strait Islander Studies – but these are not properly supported. There is a yawning gulf between the work they are able to do and the work that needs to be done.

Australia does not have a comprehensive agenda for the recording, preservation, presentation and utilisation of the country's indigenous heritage. The urgent work, described by Rachel Perkins, of recording the songlines of central Australia is just one example of the work that needs to be done Before It's Too Late (BITL).

The former director of the then Australian Institute of Aboriginal Studies, the late English archaeologist Peter Ucko, was the architect of the first BITL push, which saw scores of young anthropologists and linguists deployed to the four corners of the continent to undertake salvage work by making indigenous language and ethnographic recordings. This work captured the knowledge of the last of the old people born in the bush, before the mission era. Some of Australia's leading anthropologists, such as Peter Sutton, were part of this drive.

Australia urgently needs a BITL Mark 3, since the generation that worked on the cattle stations, who were brought up and worked on the land, and who learnt the languages – the next generation on from the old bush-born generation – are now old and passing on. Much of this knowledge will be lost if we do not grasp the importance and urgency of this work. Also, the work compiled by that first generation of BITL researchers needs to be the subject of urgent work itself: converting the mouldering contents of storage rooms of ethnographers who are now in their seniority into forms that are accessible and useful to future generations. It is no exaggeration to say that the notebooks and journals of the researchers who worked in Cape York Peninsula these past fifty years are themselves part of the world's heritage. We need concerted public support to secure this heritage. And of course much more recording work, utilising the latest information technology, lies ahead of new generations of linguists and ethnographers. The universities need to be part of this national drive over the coming decades, because they need to provide the personnel for this drive.

In 2001, the world watched aghast as the Taliban dynamited and destroyed the 1700-year-old Buddhas of Bamiyan in Afghanistan. Treasures of older lineage are in danger of being lost to our nation through blindness and neglect rather than vandalism.

MAKING PEACE

> We have to make peace with the Aboriginal people.
> — Prime Minister Paul Keating,
> address to staff, election eve, 1993

> Australia is a blessed country. Our climate, our land, our people, our institutions rightly make us the envy of the earth; except for one thing – we have never fully made peace with the first Australians.
> — Leader of the Opposition Tony Abbott,
> second reading of the *Aboriginal and
> Torres Strait Islanders Recognition Bill*, 2013

The national challenge we have embarked upon is the task of getting the majority of the voters in a majority of the states to say yes. This is not a simple majority. Constitutional reform will not just happen because we get 51 per cent of the country on board. Once, 65 per cent of the country voted for a change and it did not get up, because under our constitution the formula for an amendment is a majority of voters in a majority of states. It cannot just be for a progressive cause: it has to be a liberal cause; it has to be a conservative cause if you want amendment. Our forebears who brought about the 1967 referendum understood that, and they achieved the most handsome vote in favour of changing the constitution when 90 per cent of the country voted in favour of indigenous citizenship.

We want to repeat that achievement. We have got to bring the whole country on board. We cannot just seek the endorsement of friends and allies. That is the easy strategy: to talk to those who readily support us. The challenge is to gather in conservatives and Liberals and people with genuine anxieties about amending what is a foundational document.

We must respect conservative concerns about the constitution. But my argument to the conservatives is ultimately that you cannot have a unified nation, this cannot be a fair nation, without the proper inclusion of that

3 per cent of the nation who were originally excluded from the constitution. And who, when belatedly acknowledged in 1967, were included on the fatefully wrong basis of race.

So our task is cut out for us, but all the indications from polling show that the great majority of Australians want recognition of this country's original people in the constitution. We start with a very deep reservoir of goodwill. And for those of us who believe it is important that indigenous Australians have a rightful place in this their own nation, the challenge over the coming period is to engage the rest of the country.

The journey of reform and inclusion is never quick. Consider how long the United States took to get from the Declaration of Independence to the Emancipation Proclamation under Lincoln, and then to Martin Luther King's achievement of civil rights. Many decades lay between each of these milestones in the history of their republic, and much suffering.

The Australian Constitution is 113 years old. We still do not have a proper foundation for recognising indigenous Australians. It is a long time in the history of our country for this business not to be finished. I hope that the rest of the country, contemplating these reforms, will understand that the suffering and exclusion will continue for as long as we don't perfect the basis of our citizenship. And make a more complete commonwealth.

John Edwards

There is much to reflect upon in Andrew Charlton's wide-ranging and beguilingly written essay. He argues that China's demand for resources has been very important to Australia's prosperity in recent years, and that the growth in China's demand for resources is likely to be weaker in coming years. No disagreement there. He also argues that Australia needs to have a flexible economy, attend to the education and training of its workforce, expand its services exports and encourage innovation. Again, no disagreement. I do disagree with him, however, on how Australia has responded to the mining boom, and therefore on where we are now and where we go next. In *Beyond the Boom*, published around the same time as Charlton's essay, I come to quite different conclusions.

For example, a central point of Charlton's essay is that "Australians did not save much of the proceeds of the mining boom over the past decade." This is an important argument, and much leads from it. But as I show in *Beyond the Boom*, there is another way to think about our experience. Since the boom in resource prices got going at the end of 2003, Australia's national savings have increased by 3 per cent of GDP, to one quarter of GDP. Almost all of the increase has been in household savings. About half of the increase occurred before the global financial crisis, and half afterwards. The significance of this 3 per cent is that it is equal to the Australian resident share of the increase in mining export revenues over the same period. Far from wasting the boom revenues, Australians saved them. It is certainly true that a big share of increased company tax (mostly not from mining) was handed back as personal income tax cuts, but those cuts were saved by households.

Consistent with the rising savings rate, household consumption growth during the boom has been quite restrained, particularly when compared to the previous ten years. During the boom, Australians have not only saved more and consumed less than in the decade before the boom, but also worked harder and studied more. Australia's capital stock during the boom has risen by nearly two-thirds (excluding housing), and its human capital has also increased, with more education and training. This frugal, restrained behaviour was plainly evident during and after the global financial crisis, but began earlier. One result is that Australia has financed what is probably the biggest investment boom in its history without a blowout in its current account deficit. Another is that a very big investment boom is slowing without a bust – a sharp contrast to our earlier experiences of investment booms.

In thinking about where we are and where we go next, a key issue is how big the boom has been, and whether it is over. Charlton doesn't put a number on it, but my impression is that he thinks the mining boom is very big indeed. I agree that it is big – the issue is how big. In my analysis, I show that output rose considerably faster in the ten years before the boom began than it has since, and that real incomes rose just as fast. The "boom" years have not been as good as the preceding years. Drawing on published RBA research, I estimate that the whole of the resource economy – mining, mining investment, metals processing and all the Australian inputs for these activities – rose by 3 per cent of real GDP, comparing 2012 with 2002. That is a pretty big increase, but not quite as big as commonly supposed. From 2003 to 2010, the output of mines grew as a share of GDP by the same amount as the health care and social assistance sector (both by 1 per cent of GDP). In 2010, mining was still the same share of GDP as in 1992.

More happens with Australian income, since iron ore and coal prices rose dramatically. In tracing the income gains, it's relevant that four-fifths of the mining sector is owned overseas, and half of the income from mining is attributable to overseas shareholders. The increase in Australian income due to the mining boom appears to be around 3 per cent of GDP – in this case nominal GDP and calculating the gain as the increase in the value of mining exports (or alternatively, of nominal gross value added in mining) between 2002 and 2012. Again, big – but not all that big.

So I would argue that while the boom has been extremely useful, it has not been as big as sometimes suggested, and Australia has handled it quite well. Nor is the boom by any means over – mining output has only accelerated markedly faster than GDP over the past few years. There is plenty more to come in increased iron ore output, and the big increase in LNG exports hasn't yet begun.

What is passing is the crest of the mining investment boom. In 2003, mining investment was around 2 per cent of GDP and today it is around 8 per cent. We might expect mining investment to get back to 2 or 3 per cent of GDP in the next three or four years. But half of the goods and services in mining investment are imported, so the drag on Australian GDP or the amount we need to replace is around 3 per cent of GDP. That will be difficult, but by no means impossible. Increased mining output will help, as will increased home construction – and there is plenty of evidence both are occurring. There is also room for increased household consumption and increased infrastructure investment. Business investment outside mining has been weak since the global financial crisis. At some point it will pick up.

Charlton argues that Australia has been afflicted with the "Dutch Disease," by which increased resource exports come at the expense of the rest of the economy. This is certainly widely believed, and often repeated. The Dutch Disease mechanism depends on a limited supply of capital and labour, which is then allocated away from activities such as services or manufacturing, and towards mining. But in a relatively small open economy without capital controls there is no constraint on capital, other than the rate of return. The capital invested in mining is not capital that might otherwise be profitably invested in manufacturing or farming or finance. At least half of the inputs into mining investment and mining are imported. Nor is labour closely constrained. In the first ten years of the boom, Australia added a net two million migrants to its population – a high proportion of them workers. The mining and construction workforces have increased during the boom, but even so the whole of the increase in both sectors is no more than one-fifth of the increase in the total number of employees in Australia from the beginning of the boom until now. Evidently, we can run a mining boom without shutting down the rest of the place.

It's true that the relatively high dollar has lowered returns in export industries from what they might otherwise be (including, of course, returns from mining exports). The issue is how big the effect has been. What we can say with certainty is that in December last year the number of short-term visitor arrivals (mostly tourists) to Australia reached a new peak of well over three-quarters of a million, and that in seasonally adjusted terms tourist arrivals are running this year at a record level that is one-third higher than it was before the mining boom began. That should cheer Charlton's gloomy Cairns café owner, Darren. Farm exports in the year to May were more than two-thirds up compared to the first year or so of the boom. Education exports have rebounded to a new high that is more than double the level at the beginning of the boom. Service exports overall are now running at a level more than two-thirds higher than before the boom. These are all current dollar increases, which is a relevant measure if we are thinking about the impact of a higher exchange rate. Exports of manufactures (excluding metals) haven't done so well, but they are up by over a third in

Australian dollars, and in volume terms are up by one quarter compared to their level when the boom began. All up, the dollar value of exports, excluding all mining and metals exports, is up by half as much again compared to the beginning of the boom in 2003. So if we have Dutch Disease, it's a pretty mild case. (The same goes for imports. In theory we should have vastly increased consumer imports; in practice we haven't.)

Charlton raises some dire predictions on the outlook for China, and then qualifies them. As he writes, the Chinese leadership is well aware of the issues and is addressing them through faster wage increases, some financial liberalisation, and so forth. China has, he rightly says, a considerable buffer in the form of vast currency reserves and, one might add, in a savings rate that could be a lot lower without damage to the China economy. And, as he also writes, there are instances of interminable crises in recent history, but there are also plenty of instances of managed transitions. On this issue, I am with Charlton the optimist rather than Charlton the pessimist. We should also bear in mind that urbanisation in China has a very long way to go, and to the extent that Chinese policies favour households and consumption they will also favour home construction, since they all go together. New towns and cities, with new apartment blocks, use a lot of steel.

Finally, it is not at all central to Charlton's argument, but I often wonder whether his interpretation of the global financial crisis – which is the same as that of Ben Bernanke, Joe Stiglitz and plenty of others – is completely convincing. Basically, in this interpretation China is to blame by causing a "savings glut." This reasoning implies that intended global saving in the years preceding the financial crisis was higher than intended global investment. If that was the case, and the United States was a preferred destination for this excess, one would expect to see US interest rates falling and the US dollar rising as savers compete to buy US dollar assets. But when one looks at the numbers, it is not so. In the five years before the global financial crisis, US interest rates were rising – both short term and long term. At the same time the US dollar was falling. Against the Chinese yuan, for example, it fell by more than a tenth. These price movements are in quite the wrong direction for the "savings glut" story. Furthermore, US household consumption rose no faster than GDP in the years of the global financial crisis, while exports and business investment grew very much faster. Those facts do not fit the "savings glut" story either. The glut explanation has the happy property of finding China at fault for exporting cheap manufactures and buying US treasury bonds. US investment banks were thus unwitting victims of this macroeconomic mystery. There is of course much more in this debate, but

I am unconvinced by Charlton's presentation of what I readily concede is a widely respected view.

Charlton's interpretation of the boom years is of a piece with his interpretation of Australian economic history. Here he retells the familiar story of a "Federation Settlement" of high wages, high tariffs and restricted immigration to make a case that Australia's comparative performance declined from around 1890 to the early 1980s, when it was reformed by the Hawke and Keating governments. This is a big issue, but any reader who has got this far deserves a break. Those interested in a different and I think more plausible view of Australia's economic history might profitably read Ian McLean's wonderful book *Why Australia Prospered*, which I draw on in *Beyond the Boom*. McLean's title suggests the difference between his interpretation of Australian economic history and the black armband story recounted by Charlton.

I have disagreements, but I should also say that I think Charlton has made a valuable contribution to the Australian economic debate by tackling some big themes in a thoughtful way. There is much in his Quarterly Essay that I found stimulating.

John Edwards

Max Corden

Dragon's Tail is an excellent, colourful review of the China boom and its effects on the Australian economy. The boom has brought in lots of income to Australians, partly from governments getting revenue through corporation tax and royalties. It is estimated that about half of the total gains from the boom (measured as value added) went to foreign shareholders of the mining companies. This seems excessive, and could have been reduced by higher taxation at the high-boom stage. The boom has also had the adverse side effect of causing our exchange rate to appreciate severely, so reducing the international competitiveness of other industries: the so-called "Dutch Disease." Charlton is also right in flagging the prospect of Australia exporting more services to Asia. Perhaps, eventually, an export-of-services boom will replace the mining boom.

Here I want to discuss an issue relevant for current policy that is not widely understood, and not discussed by Charlton. My comments are influenced by information in a very interesting new book by John Edwards: *Beyond the Boom*. It contains detailed figures, derived mainly from publications of the Parliamentary Budget Office and the federal Treasury.

The boom, in the form of rising export prices for iron ore and coal, really started during the Howard government period, around 2003. As a result, corporation tax revenue unexpectedly started to increase, indeed to pour in. This went on until 2008, when the global financial crisis (GFC) hit. If there had been no changes in taxation or in government spending, the revenue would have led to a big budget surplus. Such a surplus would have been wise, because higher savings are wise when a boom is expected to be temporary and because (as Charlton notes) reduced spending would moderate the Dutch Disease problem.

But, perhaps unwisely, the Howard government cut taxes with a series of successive cuts to personal income tax, flattening the tax scales and extending superannuation concessions. There was also the abolition of indexation of petroleum fuel excise. I shall call this package the "Howard Gift" – that is, the gift to the taxpaying middle and upper classes. Some budget surplus remained as a result, but then in 2008 the GFC ended the boom. There followed an increase in government spending under the Rudd government, which succeeded in avoiding a recession in Australia.

Charlton criticises the Howard government for wasting the gains of the boom. I quote: "As the boom took off between 2004 and 2007, it added $334 billion in windfall gains to the budget. Australia only saved 6 per cent of this, using the resulting 94 per cent to fund tax cuts and spending increases." This criticism of imprudence has also been made by other economists. While many (like myself) would not dispute the logic of increasing spending after 2008 to avoid a recession, the earlier Howard tax cuts and other concessions were, in retrospect, surely unwise. Possibly the Howard people thought the boom would last forever, or at least for a longer time. In fact, while the Rudd spending boom designed to avoid recession was temporary, the Howard tax cuts and related measures were meant to be permanent and hence turned out to be a time bomb that exploded later.

But now I come to an important point made by Edwards in his book. What happened to private savings at that time? It turns out that private household savings increased so much that, it seems, the whole of the extra income from the tax cuts and more was saved. To some extent this was motivated by the GFC. Australians, as private citizens, saved so much that a large part of the increased business investment at that time was financed from within Australia and not from abroad. We may have had an imprudent Coalition government, but we, the people, were appropriately cautious.

I now come to my main point relevant for current policy.

After a year, the Rudd spending boom came to an end. Government spending as a proportion of GDP started declining, but big budget deficits emerged because government revenue was going down. This was a Labor (Gillard) government period and – contrary to accusations – the budget deficits were not caused by increased spending by an irresponsible Labor government. These deficits were a result of the time bomb of the Howard Gift, the delayed effects of the earlier tax cuts and related measures.

The Abbott government has claimed that its budget deficit problem has been inherited from Labor. That is literally true because Labor deficits preceded the current potential deficits. But the fault of Labor was not to create or increase its deficits with extra spending, but rather to fail to reverse the imprudent Howard Gift. In view of the then Opposition's campaign against tax increases, a reversal of the Howard Gift by Labor would presumably have been politically impossible.

And here is my conclusion. This is solely my conclusion, not Edwards'. The Howard tax cuts were understandably motivated by the favourable budget effects of the unexpected big boom in export prices. *But the boom turned out to be temporary, so the Howard Gift should also be temporary.* It should now be reversed. Taxes should be increased. Since both Government and Opposition are concerned about future budget deficits, this should be a bipartisan decision. The joint decision about the needed tax increases should be made now, to be implemented gradually. To avoid endless arguments (and lobbying) about the details, the whole of the Howard Gift, neither more nor less, should be reversed. Increases in taxation would be less costly to Australian society than some of the other measures on the expenditure side being currently implemented or proposed.

Max Corden

Michael Cooney

When Andrew Charlton "came back" to Australia – do they do that anywhere else? – he had a Rhodes scholarship, an Oxford doctorate, a co-author credit with a Nobel laureate, and he'd worked at the UN, the OECD and the LSE. He was two years older than Germaine Greer was when she left Australia.

And in that year of miracles, 2007, the only greater wonder than this CV was that he had a book under his arm that was helpful to the Australian Labor Party. The contrast with the books written by former and future Labor frontbenchers in the preceding decade was morally impressive. Mature leaders such as Latham and Tanner had mixed creative and constructive new ideas with a pervasive "What do we stand for?" angst. Widely admired figures such as Button and Jones, who'd made their lives and livings in the movement, had spent their retirements throwing stones at us. Here was a kid of my generation who was prepared to throw stones at the other side.

The big thing about Charlton's *Ozonomics* was its explicit attack on Australian conservative economic management. In fact the book was subtitled *Inside the Myth of Australia's Economic Superheroes* and the cover showed a comic pairing of Prime Minister Howard and Treasurer Costello as "Mr Fantastic" and "Mr Boombastic". And Charlton was right.

What made this genuinely fresh wasn't just that it was an attack on the right's failures of economic management. It was also a last, late flowering of a *Labor* account of the much-chronicled "reform era" of Australian politics, before the seeming final triumph of the bipartisan myth. Bagging the Tories of the mid-2000s was one thing. Bagging the Tories of the mid-1980s was quite another. And by no means did Charlton do this when it was fashionable or easy. The book was written in what Kim Beazley used to call the "dog days of opposition." All you could say was bravo, and can we host a book event for you?

Even more remarkable, Andrew then went to work for the Labor Party, and for Australia, and did some pretty amazing things.

So when a bloke who wrote almost the only helpful book in eleven years of opposition and who's been a G20 sherpa says he has a warning for you, you stop and listen. And in *Dragon's Tail*, Andrew Charlton has a warning for us:

> If we are happy to leave our prosperity to luck, we can continue to bob up and down on the tide of global circumstance; but if we want to be a successful country, we need to learn to surf the waves.

It's hard to disagree, in that it's hard to argue for an approach that relies more on luck. But do we really not know how to "surf the waves" now? Let me put the objection another way. Charlton asks if we want to "be" a successful country, but shouldn't this be: if we want to *stay* a successful country?

I hope this isn't only wounded pride from someone who never left. I hope my real problem with a warning against second-rate leadership and popular complacency isn't that it's obviously false, but rather that it's obviously true. I don't disagree with Andrew, I just want him to be less general; I want more explanatory power. When he writes:

> We haven't helped ourselves … In the boom years, Australians embraced the windfall of China's growth without preparing for the aftermath. We allowed the non-mining economy to wither and failed to save resources profits. As a nation, we have to be smarter than this.

I think of my father's ancient joke about the Lone Ranger and Tonto, surrounded by hostile "Indians".

> Lone Ranger: Tonto, I think we're in trouble
> Tonto: What's this "we" shit, white man?

Because if Australians, and our leaders, are going to act on Andrew's warning, we need an explanation of problems of national leadership which doesn't occlude politics. We need to know the detail of the problems. Because actually, *we* didn't spend the boom windfall on a lower top tax rate for our mates, superannuation tax breaks for our wives, school rifle ranges for our kids and a Middle East war for some poor bastard in Darwin or Townsville – *they* did. The problem isn't the quality of Australian political leadership; the problem is the quality of

Australian *conservative* leadership. Even where progressives have "failed," it's been a failure precisely to overcome conservative resistance to our ideas. Failing to beat the bad guys is a kind of culpability, especially when it's your job to beat them, but it's a very different kind from actually being the bad guys.

Charlton gets this, of course – in fact, he's lived it as much as anyone. He's got as many scars as Coriolanus. So yes, much of his discussion implicitly accounts for the big differences between how Australia was governed before 1996 and how it was governed between 1996 and 2007 and then how it was governed between 2007 and 2013. It's not an error not to whack a party bumper sticker on this part of his discussion – but the decision not to do so demands something of the reader.

"He who has ears to hear, let him hear." You have to see through the non-partisan economic presentation to the political facts. Don't be fooled by the respectability of this account. Read between the lines.

Looking for the real politics in the story of national leadership becomes even more important when Andrew's wider argument about Australian economic history comes into play, because here I think he is importantly wrong. While his account of post-1983 economics is close to silent on politics but consistent with a sound political analysis, his account of the "long history" really does miss the mark. He writes:

> The long history of our economy can be summed up in a single sentence: Australia had a very good nineteenth century, a poor twentieth century and a stellar start to the twenty-first century.

No, we didn't. In fact, Andrew's own data and chart prove him wrong.

On page 12, the chart "Australia's global rank" shows "Australia's position in the world's richest countries measured by GDP per capita" from 1825 to 2012. On this chart Australia's global rank sits at ninth in 1895. We tick up a couple of places, and then down a couple of places, for the next *sixty-five years*. On Andrew's data, Australia is eleventh in the world in 1960. That's a lifetime of holding our own.

We then crash to twenty-first in the world in 1988. The bars on Andrew's chart show this perfectly clearly.

This is the key point. Australia held its place from ninth to eleventh for sixty-five years through a depression and two world wars – and then we fell from eleventh to twenty-first in less than twenty-five.

But Andrew bangs across the top of this chart a giant arrow that points down for a hundred years. This makes the catastrophe of the 1890s financial collapses and subsequent depression (when we pretty much went from first to ninth in one mad Collins Street afternoon) look like a steady decline running for the next six decades. So what should be a long flat line from Federation onwards is an arrow going down at thirty degrees. This is even more confusing because the horizontal axis gives the same amount of space to the period 1905 to 1960 as it does the period 1960 to 1988. So the visual representation of the decline after 1960 should point downwards twice as steeply as it does. What should be an arrow pointing at sixty degrees looks only half as steep.

So across this chart, we see a long decline from 1885 to 1988. What we should see instead is something like two hands of a clock, with the long minute hand pointing to nine and the short hour hand pointing to five, centred on the year 1961.

If we did, then we would see that Australia didn't have a "bad century" which started with the Harvester judgment. Australia had a "lost generation" which started with the credit squeeze.

I don't think for a moment Andrew is trying to trick us – for a start, I'm sure that the single biggest explanation for the apparent distortion here is how wide the page is and how many data points were available. But I do think this chart is incredibly revealing. It's not a great illustration of what happened in Australia, but it's a perfect picture of what many people think happened in Australia in the twentieth century, and a striking proof that even the most striking economic data can't counter this fixed view.

The real lesson is that so many of us, including Andrew, are trapped in a myth about what went on in the politics of Australia before 1983 and what the real economic problem was before Hawke and Keating. Because that arrow has an author – that idea of a bad twentieth century has a parent – and it's not Andrew Charlton, and it's not Paul Keating either, it's Paul Kelly.

And Paul Kelly is wrong.

And that matters.

It matters because if you accept the big myth of the "bad century" (the long decline from Harvester onwards), the trifecta favoured by Andrew here, and by so many in Ross Garnaut's "independent centre" – of micro-flexibility, revenue stability and productivity growth – isn't enough. You end up deciding that we have to chuck out the whole progressive Australian model of a stable economy and moderate social protections, and you end up convinced that we have to start with industrial relations.

But we don't want to, we don't need to, and in fact to do so would make us all worse off. On the other hand, if you recognise the reality of the "lost generation" (the steep decline from 1961), you see something quite different. The longstanding centrist economic approach, combined with a serious progressive political effort to ensure the benefits flow to all, can get us where we want to go. We just need not to slip back into the way Menzies and his successors did business for a relatively brief period from 1961 to 1983.

What does that mean in practice? Well, start with this fact. The years 1960 to 1985 weren't decades of Keynesianism and egalitarianism gone rogue. They were a golden age of rent-seeking at the top end of town.

What does that period tell you about the politics of today? About who to trust on corporate tax adequacy? Or about who to listen to in the financial sector? Or about what is good support to regional communities and what is blunt subsidy in agribusiness? Or about who can manage the US alliance as an asset in Asia? It's not a story that Maurice Newman or Tony Shepherd probably want to hear. But it is a story that a lot of smart people – in business, in universities, in government, in community leadership – can apply to the real challenges for Australia today.

Not only of Asia, but also of ageing, clean energy, new jobs, future growth.

Instead, today, we're led by crass conservatives such as Abbott and Hockey, feeble liberals such as Hunt and Turnbull, and ludicrous populists such as Joyce. They've made Peter Costello's adjournment debate clichés in his News Ltd tabloid columns look economically sophisticated; they've made John Howard's family tax policies look practical and fair. Australia is in far greater danger of being governed as we were in the 1960s than as we were in the 1900s or the 1940s. The threat to our ability to adapt successfully to a changing China and a changing world isn't a return to type by the Australian left, it's a return to type by the Australian right.

If the argument goes astray with that graph on page 12, it finds its line and length again with the postcard view of "Pudong transformed" that Andrew shares with us on page 18.

Dragon's Tail is really a story about the Australia we could have if we're governed well – one which is prosperous and inclusive, and yes, one which is smart, sceptical and unsentimental about China. It's really an essay about whether our leaders settle for fragile prosperity based on a boom and growing inequality, or whether they aim for us to remain a rich, fair, stable country – and to become more like that over time.

In this respect, it's an essay about how much of Australia's future is explained by that view in Shanghai. Yes, it is one of the most important and impressive sights in the world – and yes, it symbolises change in Australia as well as in

China. I've been lucky enough to see it a few times in the past ten years and the wow won't wear off before I see it next.

The last time I was there, Prime Minister Gillard was announcing one of the biggest deals for the Australian finance sector so far in the young Asian Century – licensing Westpac and ANZ to trade the Australian dollar and the Chinese yuan directly in mainland China. This is one of the big openings to service exports that Andrew rightly points to as the future for us in China and Asia.

That was on a very short visit in April 2013. We arrived late evening from Hainan, stayed in a hotel on the Bund and left next morning for Beijing. So there was only going to be a brief opportunity to feast on the view from high in the hotel. But we'd got in after 10 p.m. and it was too late. There were power cuts across the river and the lights were out – even on the Oriental Pearl. We had a drink in the dark.

Michael Cooney

Jim Chalmers

Thankfully, the argument playing out in elite publications like this one about the nature of Australia's past, present and future economy is far more civilised and sophisticated in tone than some of the arguments that Andrew Charlton and I had as young staffers in the offices of a former prime minister and treasurer. Back in the first Rudd government, "Sandy" had the frustrating ability to change his boss's mind after a policy debate had already been carried out and won. In this respect, Charlton was to the Rudd prime ministership what Valerie Jarrett reportedly is to the Obama presidency: an indispensable adviser in the envied yet generally unpopular position at the absolute centre of the leader's Venn diagram of influence.

Dragon's Tail shows that Charlton has lost none of the writing skill and sharp observations of his time in the service of government. Nor has he lost his interest in the big economic debates shaping the country or his willingness to engage in them, despite having begun a promising career in the private sector. This is a well-written, well-motivated discussion of the Australian economy, its connectedness with China's and the flow-on impacts on the Australian dollar and Australian commodities and what this means for our competitiveness. It should be read alongside John Edwards' brilliant *Beyond the Boom*, which asks some of the same questions and yet offers some very different answers.

Before I had even torn the plastic off my copy of *Dragon's Tail*, I took an excited call from an astute and experienced observer of Australia's political economy, who pointed me towards the captivating graph on page 12. Adapting material provided by Angus Maddison, Charlton graphs Australia's relative rank in the world, measured by GDP per capita: effectively, wealth or economic activity per person. It looks a bit like an "N": Australia climbs from eleventh to first between 1825 and 1885, drops to twenty-first in 1988, and climbs back to seventh by 2012. Summarised: "Australia had a very good nineteenth century, a poor twentieth century and a stellar start to the twenty-first century." Agriculture explains our early success, but lacklustre competitiveness and protectionist economic tendencies saw us languish for much of the century that followed the remarkable late-1800s peak as the world's richest economy per capita.

International comparisons have their limits, of course, as Edwards points out and as a Coalition backbencher discovered when criticised for comparing Australian inequality with the situation in the developing countries of Asia. But what makes them so useful for Charlton's Quarterly Essay is that comparing Australian wealth per person with the rest of the world over time gives us a useful picture of the rise and fall of the Australian economy and the influence of the domestic policy environment. More than that, it demonstrates that boom times in trade are not the whole story of Australia's performance. If they were, as well as the "wool" peak of 1885, the graph would show another in the early 1950s, and then a "mining" peak in the first two-thirds of the 2000s.

That brings me to two partisan observations that Charlton can't or won't make as an aspiring corporate titan (and that Edwards can't or won't make as a member of the Reserve Bank Board). The first is that the sharpest decline in Australia's relative economic strength began under Menzies, while the sharpest improvement was bookended by the Hawke–Keating program of economic reform and the world-beating Rudd–Gillard–Swan stimulus program (which accounts for the biggest jump over three years in the graph, from sixteenth in 2006 to eleventh in 2009).

The second political point is again about the usefulness of comparisons to give context to domestic data. As a first-term member of parliament, I have lost count of the number of occasions – be it during Question Time or in one of the many opportunities to debate Coalition counterparts on twenty-four-hour news channels – that Labor's political opponents have cited figures from the period 2007–13 in isolation, ignoring entirely the sharpest downturn in the global economy since the Great Depression. Yes, the unemployment rate was higher at the end of the Rudd–Gillard period than at the beginning. Of course it was. But everyone involved in the debate knows that Australian unemployment rose by a fraction of that in comparable countries. Australia and the United States began the crisis with similar levels of unemployment and yet unemployment in the United States peaked at almost twice that in Australia. And yes, Australian growth softened. But as the Charlton–Maddison graph shows, we leapt ten positions in the global ranking over the course of the Labor government.

So, in an increasingly connected global economy, comparisons matter and facts matter. And so does government policy. Like Charlton and Edwards, I have never believed in command and control economic policy. As I said in my first parliamentary speech, I don't pretend that the decisions of governments are all that matter, or even most of what matter. Charlton's book *Ozonomics* went to great lengths to demonstrate that under Howard and Costello our economy largely drove itself. But to ignore the role of policy would be to ignore the role Hawke and Keating played in opening Australia up to the world. It would deny the potential impacts of the current government's attack on human capital investment. And it would disown the obvious successes of Labor's stimulus during the global financial crisis.

This is where Charlton disappoints. It is one thing to omit the partisan points that politicians will pick up. It is entirely another to write such a long piece with hardly any reference to the stimulus packages and no mention at all of resource taxation or the role of superannuation in building national savings. In an essay about the relationship of our reliance on resources exports to China, a historically high dollar and what was popularly described as a two-speed economy, this defies explanation. Charlton was key to all of these considerations in the first Rudd government, and his insights into these specific areas of policy would add to his essay. Instead, he has volunteered for witness protection! Beginning a new career is one thing; pretending you never had the old one is another.

Nonetheless, *Dragon's Tail* has already penetrated deep into the thinking of economists and policy-makers, if the copies spotted at a recent conference at ANU's Crawford School conference of Public Policy are anything to go by. This is a good thing. Anyone who bemoans the day-to-day political and economic commentary would welcome a contribution as thoughtful as this. Little wonder Charlton is so often mentioned – including in Mark Latham's review in the *Australian Financial Review* – as someone who could make a big contribution to the Australian Labor Party if and when his career takes another turn.

Jim Chalmers

Eric Knight

Andrew Charlton's Dragon's Tail is a sharp analysis of what is happening inside Australia's most significant trade partner. His insight into China's unsustainable investment-led growth model is spot-on, and we have good reason to worry about the flow-on effects for Australia. Where the essay is weakest is on the specific alliances and mechanisms needed to diversify Australia's industrial base and increase our international competitiveness. Also missing from these pages is the question of power: which figures have the political capital and public standing to pursue a productivity agenda and actually make it happen?

Power lies at the heart of any visionary economic change. It is especially important when it comes to micro-economic reform, because such changes intimately affect employment, jobs and wages. They require re-skilling, radical new work practices and clever integration of technology. Politicians must attend to contradictory demands: they must reassure voters that they have our best interests at heart (the public interest ethic), while simultaneously asking people to change their livelihoods (the market ethic). Charlton's essay captures the macro shift governing Australia's economic future (China–Australia), but misses this micro, more human, one.

Through the 1980s and '90s, the Hawke–Keating government was able to drive reform by leveraging its close relationship with organised labour. In the early 1980s, when Hawke came to power, 50 per cent of Australian workers were trade union members. This gave Bill Kelty and others the power and authority they needed to negotiate with the government and tackle difficult labour-market reform through the Prices and Incomes Accord. Today this powerbase is fragmented, with only 17 per cent unionised and the vast majority of workers independently organised, with little connection to or interest in unions. This highlights why the current reform agenda is less cohesive and harder to pursue. The country lacks a set of leaders or an interest group that commands this space as one did in the 1980s.

Someone or something needs to fill this power vacuum if we are to make progress towards a more flexible labour market that can strike the right balance between business as usual and the riskier, entrepreneurial ventures that create genuinely new jobs. Charlton implicitly turns to an alliance between Canberra and big business as an exemplar. The essay opens with Kevin Rudd marching into a room in Australia's Beijing embassy, taking a seat alongside Marius Kloppers (BHP), Tom Albanese (Rio Tinto) and Andrew Forrest (Fortescue) to negotiate for our resource interests. Charlton argues that Rudd is Australia's "Manchurian Candidate," a man able to "bring Australia into China's orbit" and navigate "around the political barriers to a closer economic relationship." This sounds impressive, but the encounter reads more as the miners getting free lobbying assistance from our prime minister than a reform discussion in the public interest.

Abbott is pursuing a similar tack, and his government is now experiencing the shortcomings of this approach. Big business has shown that it can run a negative campaign (for example, against the mining tax) but is yet to prove it can run a positive one that can sell significant, bipartisan economic reform. Abbott is in a strange place now, because he has bet on big business being his emissary and he is frustrated by its failure to deliver. Abbott vented his frustration at the recent B20 conference in Sydney: "The lesson of previous reforms here in Australia and elsewhere is that business must be an advocate in the court of public opinion for policies that encourage trade, strengthen the economy and adhere to sound business principles." Since the defeat of WorkChoices, there is a lingering feeling among Coalition MPs that big business has not done enough to sell big economic reform.

Big business may have been a weak public advocate, but it has been a direct private beneficiary. The Australian Bureau of Statistics and the Australian Productivity Commission show that mining, financial services, utilities and manufacturing have led the country's decline in total productivity since 2007. For example, productivity in the mining sector has fallen between 8 and 10 per cent annually for the last three years. These sectors also happen to be among the country's most heavily subsidised. At a time when the government is asking health care and education to bear the brunt of fiscal austerity, the subsidies to big business are baffling. In 2012 alone, financial services ($640 million), mining ($547 million) and motor vehicles and parts ($461 million) received an array of generous subsidies from tax concessions and hand-outs. According to the Australian Productivity Commission, these totalled about $7.8 billion last year across thirty-four industries.

If Australia is to have a genuine, comprehensive dialogue on productivity, competitiveness and entrepreneurship, it needs a new partner to rally the country and frame the political narrative. My view is that this partner ought to be the non-school education sector. This sector is better placed than any other to balance the public interest by creating a more flexible, internationally competitive workforce. Although few Australians are aware of it, education is the country's fourth largest industry by export revenue after iron ore, coal and gold, and is the largest service-based industry. The institutions where we are educated are the ones with which we are most likely to have an enduring relationship, and which we are most likely to have in common with others. Fifty-seven per cent of the population aged fifteen to sixty-four hold non-school educational qualifications, and this figure rises to 69 per cent among those who have completed Year 12. It includes our universities, but also our TAFEs and other professional providers. Through international students, education is also the main gateway for skilled migration into the country: 500,000 international students were enrolled in Australia last year.

The 1980s saw Australia's workforce move from being unionised to non-unionised at the same time that it shifted from being often untrained to consistently trained. We need to extend the implications of this shift politically to increase the sector's responsibility and power to create public policy. If productivity is ultimately about boosting output, then the education sector exerts an important influence by: (1) training our school graduates to have dynamic, flexible careers; (2) retraining workers whose careers have stalled so they can find better jobs; and (3) attracting the world's best skilled migrants, educating them and giving them opportunities to stay and work. The education sector also intersects with areas such as infrastructure investment, cultural engagement and migration, the commercialisation of research and development, and new construction, housing, retail and tourism.

At a recent event with Bob Hawke, John Howard cautioned today's politicians not to underestimate the ability of Australians to digest a detailed argument. A master of building and deploying power, he argued that Australians "will respond to an argument for change and reform [but] they want two requirements. They want to be satisfied it's in the national interest, because they have a deep sense of nationalism and patriotism. They also want to be satisfied it's fundamentally fair." These are well-timed comments. The country lacks a power base from which to shape a reform agenda on productivity, entrepreneurship and skills which can bring disparate interests together and make a case that is market-led, ambitious and fair.

Eric Knight

Billy Griffiths

A new body of Australian literature has emerged from the boom: it tells us that we are living in extraordinary times and that this is "The Australian Moment." But is this "The Sweet Spot," or the "Great Australian Complacency?" Have we made our own luck, or are we suffering from "Too Much Luck?" Can we stride "Beyond the Boom," or are the "Dog Days" already upon us? Above all, this new wave of national introspection asks: what are the challenges facing "the Lucky Country after the China Boom?"

Andrew Charlton's essay *Dragon's Tail* is a fine new contribution to the genre. He shares the collective fascination with Australia's sustained prosperity – indeed he regards this as "perhaps the most important question facing our nation" – and he, too, senses that our next steps are critical. But Charlton avoids the triumphalism that often marks this genre and instead highlights the outside forces that have shaped Australia. He warns against taking favourable global circumstances for granted. And he urges us to understand the remarkable transformations taking place in China.

But what of the diplomatic challenges that lie ahead? *Dragon's Tail* opens with a banquet in Beijing in 2008. It is a tense affair. The Chinese diners feel ambushed by recent demands made by the Australian mining executives sitting across from them, while the Australians have concerns about China's foreign investment strategy of "going out." Despite the friction at the table, the diners understand the importance of this relationship. They sit together and swap pleasantries. Eventually, the prime minister of Australia bounds into the room and greets the company – in fluent Mandarin. The banquet is a powerful illustration of how far Australia and China have come in such a short time, and how much we have to lose.

Australia's contemporary diplomatic relationship with China was forged decades earlier at a time of extreme domestic and international hostility towards

China. Gough Whitlam courted the Chinese from opposition, travelling with a small delegation of Australians to a closed China in 1971. He was the first Western leader to do so. One member of the delegation, Graham Freudenberg, later stressed the improbability of the enterprise: "If a fortune-teller had told me at the beginning of 1971 that I would go either to China or the moon that year, I would have opted for the moon as the more probable destination." Whitlam hoped the visit would mark the end of Australian thinking about China in terms of red and yellow perils. On crossing the border in 1971, he boldly declared to the accompanying press: "Australia will learn more about China in the next 14 days than ever previously." The 1971 visit was an inspired act of diplomacy and the product of Whitlam's sustained campaign to recognise China, but he was responding to an immediate crisis in the wheat trade.

During the 1950s and '60s Australia developed a lucrative trade in wheat and wool with China. The contrasting images of "China the traditional enemy" and "China the good customer" were balanced with the firm assertion that Australia did not mix trade and politics. In October 1970 Canada extended political recognition to China. Australia's wheat contracts abruptly stopped, while Canada's trade blossomed. Two years later, the newly elected Whitlam government officially recognised China, and Australia's wheat trade boomed. The Chinese have never shied away from using their economic weight to achieve political and strategic objectives.

The great mistake Australia made in conducting its China policy in the decades before recognition was in maintaining the mirage of China: viewing it as a political card, not a country; thinking domestically, not internationally. William McMahon, prime minister in 1971–72 and a desperate critic of Whitlam's 1971 visit, stated that China did not pay attention to statements made by "other people." But how far have we moved on from this false mentality? Michael Wesley in *There Goes the Neighbourhood* argues that Australians remain dangerously insular just as Asia has become more important than ever for national prosperity and security. And Charlton laments the Australian tendency to continue to look at national issues "through a domestic or partisan lens."

Since coming to power in September last year, we have seen a series of diplomatic fireworks from Prime Minister Tony Abbott and Foreign Minister Julie Bishop. Abbott's overtures towards Japan, in particular his bizarre decision to wade into the long-running Senkaku/Diaoyu Islands dispute, have shown an alarming lack of tact. Abbott's recent foreign policy actions bear the mark of his senior advisor on national security, Andrew Shearer, who has been characterised by Australia's first ambassador to China, Stephen FitzGerald, as "an advocate of bludgeon diplomacy and hairy-chested confrontation of China." It is a dangerous thing to compare the management of Australia's relationship with China to being able to "walk and chew gum at the same time." We should not underestimate the seriousness of the diplomatic rift that could form between the two nations.

The humiliating rebuke Bishop received in Beijing in December last year was a significant moment in the history of Australia–China relations. Before the formal closed-door meeting, in an introductory exchange usually reserved for pleasantries, China's foreign minister, Wang Yi, strongly criticised the government's foray into the East China Sea debate. With the cameras rolling, Wang declared that "what Australia has said and done with regard to [this issue] has jeopardised bilateral mutual trust and affected the sound growth of bilateral relations." The cameras were ushered out as Bishop began to respond. "I have never in thirty years encountered such rudeness," admitted Peter Rowe, the first assistant secretary of DFAT's north Asia division. FitzGerald took it a step further: "In the history of our diplomatic relations, apart from the Tiananmen massacre we've not had such a stand-off."

As the Lucky Country makes its next steps in the aftermath of the boom, it would do well to heed the advice of Andrew Charlton, Ross Garnaut and other contributors to this growing genre. But the challenges ahead are also cultural. Scholars of Australia's relations with Asia, such as Alison Broinowski, Neville Meaney and David Walker, remind us time and again that so much in cross-cultural relations hinges on perceptions, symbols and subtleties. One of the most significant slights America made against China after the rise of the Communist Party was not the trade embargo, which existed from 1949 to 1969, but rather US Secretary of State John Foster Dulles's refusal to participate in a diplomatic ritual. At the Geneva Conference in 1954, Dulles would not shake hands with the Chinese premier, Zhou Enlai. Almost twenty years later, as America was seeking a rapprochement with China, Henry Kissinger was reprimanded for this insult. When Richard Nixon finally did arrive in China in 1972, he emerged from the plane with his hand almost comically outstretched. Acts of diplomacy can have the same power as figures of trade.

Charlton calls for Australia to broaden its relationship with Asia. China's shift to a new phase of economic growth has brought the boom to an end, but China will continue to grow, and along with Japan and Asia's other growth engines – India, Indonesia and Korea – it is set to generate more diverse economic opportunities in the Asian century. We cannot afford to damage the annual leadership talks secured in April last year, or risk a downgrading of their strategic importance in Chinese eyes. Banquets are significant events. If Australia and China are yin and yang, fused together, destined to rise and fall as one, then the most disturbing of Charlton's arguments is that Australia's relationship with China – cultural as much as economic – is still poorly understood.

Billy Griffiths

Satyajit Das

Andrew Charlton's *Dragon's Tail* raises a number of important issues about Australia's prospects. "Australian exceptionalism" has been underpinned by the nation's economic performance, which has been superior to that of most developed nations, especially since the economic crisis of 2007 to 2008. There are several reasons to doubt that the nation's enviable performance can continue. It is *not* clear that policy-makers and citizens have an adequate understanding of the issues and are willing to make the difficult choices necessary.

First, Australia's enviable strong consistent economic growth, low unemployment and increasing living standards were driven by demand for commodities from emerging Asian nations, especially China. With the Middle Kingdom now accounting, directly or indirectly, for around 40 to 50 per cent of Australian exports, Australia has become the "great Southern province of China."

But Chinese growth is slowing and is structurally unsustainable, being driven by excessive reliance on debt-fuelled investment. Even if growth levels remain above those in developed markets, the changing composition of growth (a rebalancing from investment to consumption) means that resource-use intensity will decrease, reducing demand for commodities. Increased capacity, as a result of aggressive recent investment, will also come on-stream, coinciding with lower demand to put pressure on prices and volumes.

The sustainability of Australia's mineral wealth is overstated. Australia has demonstrated economic reserves of iron ore that at current production rates will last around seventy years. The comparable figures for coal and liquefied natural gas are around 100 and sixty years. But as low-cost reserves, such as the Pilbara iron ore reserves and Bowen Basin coal resources, are depleted, Australia's resource competiveness will decrease. This will be compounded by the country's high cost structures and its poor record of cost escalation, which will encourage investors to look elsewhere. Exports of some commodities, such as coal, may be adversely affected by measures to reduce carbon emissions.

A second reason for concern is that the commodity boom, Australia's role as an investment proxy for China, its AAA-rated safe-haven status and relatively higher interest rates have increased the value of the Australian dollar, reducing the nation's competitiveness in manufacturing, retail, tourism and exports of education and health services, which are all major employers.

Third, since 2001 Australia's trade account has been weak, despite the mining boom and record terms of trade. The nation's external finances remain weak, with a persistent current account deficit of around 3 per cent of gross domestic product, increasing the reliance on international financing.

Fourth, public finances, both national and state, are deteriorating, as strong growth in the commodity sector no longer offsets weak domestic conditions. Government revenues have deteriorated, with significant budget deficits likely.

Public finances will remain weak because of lacklustre economic activity, lack of strong employment growth, low wage increases and migration of corporate profits offshore. Longer-term structural effects such as an ageing population are major factors.

In a speech entitled "The End of the Age of Entitlement" to the Institute of Economic Affairs in London on 17 April 2012, Shadow Treasurer Joe Hockey questioned the economic sustainability of "entitlements bestowed on tens of millions of people by successive governments, fuelled by short-term electoral cycles and the politics of outbidding your opponents." It was reminiscent of an observation by former Australian Treasurer and Prime Minister Paul Keating that you cannot "get quarts from pint pots."

Hockey argued that "government spending on a range of social programs including education, health, housing, subsidised transport, social safety nets and retirement benefits [had] reached extraordinary levels as a percentage of GDP." This spending, he stated, should be funded from revenue rather than by borrowing.

In the May 2014 budget, the Coalition government sought to address the budgetary problems primarily by cutting spending. Given the political difficulties and social consequences of wholesale changes in key areas of expenditure, such as health, aged care and education, it is difficult to see how spending cuts alone can achieve the desired result. Popular resistance to cancellation of even poorly targeted welfare measures was noteworthy.

Increases in revenue are needed. This will require changes to tax bases, including increases in the goods and services tax, and adjustment of tax scales, as well as the removal of overgenerous incentives for corporate investment, retirement savings, negative gearing of real estate and taxation exemptions for residences. However, these measures are politically challenging, eliciting a high level of bipartisan caution.

Amusingly, the new government, like its predecessors on both sides of the political divide, will seek to improve its finances from efficiency dividends derived from streamlining the public sector. Given that over twenty years successive governments have taken similar initiatives, it is truly astonishing that more efficiency and cost benefits can be achieved.

Fifth, while Australia's public sector debt is manageable by global standards, household borrowing and foreign debt remains high and is likely to become an increasing constraint.

Australian household debt at the end of 2013 was around $1.8 trillion, equivalent to $80,000 per person. It has increased to around 180 per cent of household disposable income, a sharp increase from around 60 per cent in 1988 and 100 per cent in 1999. Australia's net foreign debt is around 54 per cent of GDP. Major international debt-rating agencies have repeatedly raised concerns about the nation's external liabilities, which make Australia sensitive to external financing shocks.

Sixth, the Australian banking system, while well capitalised, has a very high level of exposure to the domestic economy and the housing market, which is overvalued by most measures. A fall in real estate prices, increases in unemployment and decreases in income could expose financial system vulnerabilities.

Seventh, Australia's cost structure is high, exacerbated by the high currency. Australian minimum wages are around A$16 per hour, compared to around A$7–8 per hour in the US and A$1–2 per hour in China. The cost of Australian engineers is around A$170 per hour, compared to A$132 in the US, A$129 in the UK and A$77 in Japan. Cash costs in the mining sector have increased by over 250 per cent in the last ten years.

Improvements in productivity have been lacklustre. According to the *Global Competitiveness Report 2013–14* published by World Economic Forum, Australia has fallen to twenty-first place, dropping out of the top twenty for the first time. Arch-rival New Zealand is now ranked eighteenth in the world for competitiveness, three places above Australia.

The reality is that major structural reforms that started under prime ministers Bob Hawke and Paul Keating petered out sometime under Prime Minister John Howard.

Eighth, policy attempts to rebalance the economy have had only limited success. Australia's central bank, the Reserve Bank of Australia, has lowered interest rates to 2.5 per cent per annum, seeking to boost housing and consumption.

To date, lower rates have had a limited impact on housing, credit growth, consumption, non-commodity investment, employment and confidence. Despite recent falls, the ability to unilaterally devalue the Australian dollar remains limited. With the United States, the Eurozone, Japan, the United Kingdom and China pursuing policies designed to weaken their currencies to increase the competitiveness of their exports and reduce the purchasing power of their debts, the Australian dollar may well remain high for a long time.

A lower currency is seen by many as a solution. It may boost exports, but is dependent on external demand, which may be affected by a weak global economy. Currency weakness is a disguised attempt by policy-makers to reduce cost structures within the economy. It seeks to avoid dealing directly with labour costs, productivity and other structural problems. But its efficacy is doubtful.

As Australia is an importer of manufactured products, a lower currency will also increase prices, lowering purchasing power and damping consumption. Higher petrol prices, import costs and transportation expenses will increase a wide variety of costs, offsetting improvements in competitiveness.

Ninth, Australia's attempt to rebalance towards Asia is flawed. As the commodity and mining boom slows, Australia wants to sell food, education, health care and financial services, as well as attract Asian tourists. But Asia faces its own challenges. Australia's Asian strategy also suffers from inherent contradiction between Australia's political and defence partnership with the United States and its economic dependence on Asia. Deep-seated cultural barriers, such as the White Australia policy, which ended only in the 1970s, are ignored. Recent differences over illegal immigration highlight the problems with an Australian "pivot" towards Asia.

In the face of these factors, Australia's long-term policy options are increasingly constrained. As Australia has a largely open trading economy, policy-makers have a limited ability to influence the nation's economic future. Australia risks becoming trapped in a cycle of alternating commodity booms and domestic upswings. The latter relies on low interest rates driving real estate bubbles and "shop-till-you-drop," debt-fuelled consumption by already over-indebted households.

Efforts to wean Australia off its dependence on primary production, mineral and agriculture have had limited success. Catchy slogans such as "the clever country" and "the knowledge economy" have not reshaped the economy.

Attempts to transform Sydney into a major financial centre for Asia have been defeated by the tyranny of distance and Asian nationalism. Tourism, exports of educational, health and other services as well as intellectual property have been more successful. But a high Australian dollar and increasingly high costs threaten these industries. The decline in manufacturing and a general hollowing out of the economy also restricts future options.

The reality of recent Australian history is that the mining boom helped maintain incomes and purchasing power as the nation extracted large rewards for its mineral resources, covering up a lack of international competitiveness in many sectors, driven by high costs, poor productivity performance, declining educational achievements and a narrow industrial base.

On 29 November 2010, in a speech entitled "The Challenge of Prosperity," the governor of the Reserve Bank, Glenn Stevens, sought to illustrate the combined effect of the gains of the appreciating terms of trade position and the strength of the Australian dollar in the following way: "[In 2005] a shipload of iron ore was worth about the same as about 2,200 flat-screen television sets. [In 2010] it is worth around 22,000 flat-screen TV sets." In a Freudian slip, the governor had identified the fundamental issue with Australia's economic model.

Australia may have substantially wasted the proceeds of its mineral boom, with the proceeds channelled into consumption. In November 2012, the former treasury secretary and author of the government's Asian Century white paper, Ken Henry, mused on the intergenerational effects of Australia's economic strategy: "future generations ... will have reason to examine whether we made the most of the mining boom that we knew would not last forever."

During an interview on 19 December 2012, Glenn Stevens was asked where growth would come from to replace mining investment. He responded: "I think we always get this question: 'Where will the growth come from?' And most of the time it comes."

In a fragile and challenging international environment, the Abbott government will need to make the right policy choices and have more than the usual quota of luck to maintain the nation's stellar economic run. It is unlikely that a belief in good fortune – exemplified by Mr Micawber's confident belief that something is sure to turn up – will suffice.

Satyajit Das

Andrew Charlton

In the past two decades Australia has enjoyed extraordinary economic success. Our economy has grown no less than one-third faster than the United States', twice as fast as Europe's and three times faster than Japan's. Understanding this success is one of the most important questions for our polity, because it explains our progress and informs our plan for the future. That is why the current debate, including views from different perspectives, is very welcome indeed.

Max Corden is one of Australia's greatest international economists, known for bringing the highest academic rigour to incisive policy analysis. Corden's correspondence illuminates an important point in the current budget debate: "deficits were a result of the time bomb of the Howard Gift, the delayed effects of the earlier tax cuts and related measures," rather than the fiscal profligacy of the Labor governments. Howard had the good fortune of a gushing torrent of revenue to make his budgets look good, while Rudd and Gillard were left to watch revenue drain away as the mining boom began to fade.

John Edwards has recently made a significant contrarian contribution to the contemporary economic debate. I enjoyed his book *Beyond the Boom*, agreed with many points and learnt a lot along the way. However, Edwards' assertion that the boom made a modest contribution to Australia's economy is not correct. His main supporting statistic is that national income grew by 25 per cent in the decade 2002–12, but by 33 per cent (or 8 per cent more) in the previous decade (1992–2002). Edwards concludes that, "it is apparent the gains in the ten years before the boom began were bigger than the gains in the ten years after."

For an economist, the five scariest words in the English language are "I can't replicate your results." Edwards' preferred measure of national income is "real net national disposable income (RNNDI) per head," an Australian Bureau of Statistics series that adjusts national income for terms of trade effects, the impact of foreign ownership and the depreciation of our capital stock. Using this data, it's actually very easy to replicate Edwards' results, but not very easy to generalise them. Edwards defines the boom decade as 2002–12, but if he had chosen just one year earlier (2001–11), then the boom decade grew just as quickly as the pre-boom decade and his result disappears. Or if he had chosen any of the years before 2010, then the mining-boom period saw faster growth and his conclusion is turned on its head. The same is true of any five-year period excluding the financial crisis.

Edwards' particular conclusion is a consequence of the unusual conditions in the base year of the "pre-boom" period he selects for his comparison. Australia experienced a significant recession in 1992, which caused disposable income to fall by over 5 per cent from its peak. By starting the comparison decade from the low base of a recession, Edwards' pre-boom decade (1992–2002) looks remarkably strong and the boom decade (2002–12) appears anaemic by comparison. None of this is to say that Edwards is seeking to mislead, just that there is a danger in drawing general conclusions from snapshots of data.

Evidence for the importance of the boom is pointed out by Jim Chalmers, who criticises the Coalition for deriding Australia's economic performance over the past five years and thereby "ignoring entirely the sharpest downturn in the global economy since the Great Depression." Edwards makes the same mistake as the Coalition. Depending on how you measure it, Australia's growth before the boom may have been greater or less than the growth during the boom, but there is no doubt that Australia's performance during the boom relative to other countries was outstanding. The China boom helped Australia to thrive while other economies suffered.

Jim Chalmers writes with authority about Australia's performance during the financial crisis. He was on the quarterdeck for the 100-day battle to save Australia's economy from the global financial crisis following the fall of Lehman Brothers. At the helm of Treasurer Wayne Swan's office, Jim led one of the smartest, hardest-working and most collegial teams I have seen in any government in any country. Jim and I both remember the happy day in 2009 when we discovered that Australia had not slipped into a recession, evading the shark that had sunk its teeth into every other major advanced economy. Jim and his indefatigable team in the treasurer's office had done as much as anyone to bring that day about.

As a contemporary witness and current partisan, Jim rightly points out that Australia's rise up the global income ranking between 2007 and 2013 was facilitated by good policy from the Labor government. He refers to Labor's stimulus and superannuation policies, but could also add a wide range of other reforms and investments that made a major contribution to the success of our economy.

Michael Cooney's thoughtful contribution builds on this point, arguing that the long view of Australian economic history affirms the modern Labor model of competitive markets and investment in people. Michael argues that Australia's long decline in the twentieth century was in fact a tale of three parts: Australia declined in the early decades following the severe depression of the 1890s; Australia "held its place" in the global pecking order in the middle decades; and it suffered another steep decline in the '60s and '70s during the "golden age of rent-seeking." This triptych fits Michael's political narrative, especially his defence of the Harvester judgment's impact on Australia's economic performance in the first half of the twentieth century.

Yet Michael and I are at cross-purposes here. I do not seek to lay the blame for Australia's underperformance in the twentieth century at the feet of the Harvester judgment or any other part of the Australian Settlement. Australia's underperformance in the twentieth century was a result of declining relative labour productivity, which, over the long run and adjusted for participation, is the primary determinant of living standards. Australia's labour productivity didn't fall compared to other countries because of any particular policy; it fell because the agricultural sector (in which Australia was very efficient) shrank relative to the manufacturing and services sectors (in which Australia was less efficient). As our workforce swung away from our most productive sectors to our least productive, our productivity fell against our peers. This shift was primarily driven by technological and social forces outside the control of politics. Nonetheless, Michael and I are in agreement on the fundamental point that giving workers a decent standard of living did not cause Australia's twentieth-century decline.

I thank all the correspondents for their thoughtful contributions.

Andrew Charlton

Jim Chalmers is a Labor MP, elected at the 2013 election. Previously, he was executive director of the Chifley Research Centre, following long stints as chief of staff to Deputy Prime Minister and Treasurer Wayne Swan, senior adviser to state and federal Labor leaders, and national research manager for the Australian Labor Party. He has a PhD in political science and an honours degree in public policy. His first book, *Glory Daze*, was published in 2013.

Andrew Charlton is the author of *Ozonomics* and *Fair Trade for All* (with Joseph Stiglitz) and Quarterly Essay 44, *Man-Made World*, which won the 2012 John Button Prize. From 2008 to 2010 he was senior economic adviser to Prime Minister Kevin Rudd. He has worked for the London School of Economics, the United Nations and the Boston Consulting Group and studied at Oxford University as a Rhodes Scholar.

Michael Cooney is executive director of the Chifley Research Centre, the Australian Labor Party's think-tank. He was speechwriter to Prime Minister Julia Gillard and is the author of a forthcoming account of his time in the prime minister's office, 2010–13.

Max Corden is emeritus professor of international economics at the Johns Hopkins University, and has been a professorial fellow in the economics department of the University of Melbourne since 2002. He has been on the staff of the International Monetary Fund and a consultant for the World Bank. He has published several books and many articles on international economics, on economic development and on the Australian economy.

Satyajit Das is a Sydney-based former banker and the author of *Extreme Money* and *Traders, Guns and Money*.

John Edwards is a member of the Board of the Reserve Bank of Australia, and CEDA. He is a visiting fellow at the Lowy Institute, and an adjunct professor with the University of Sydney Business School and the John Curtin Institute of Public Policy. His most recent publication is *Beyond the Boom*. From 1997 to 2009, Dr Edwards was chief economist for Australia and New Zealand for HSBC. From 1991 to 1994, he was principal economic adviser to Treasurer and Prime Minister Paul Keating.

Billy Griffiths is a Sydney-based writer and historian. His work has appeared in Griffith REVIEW, History Magazine and Transactions of the Royal Society of South Africa. He is the author of The China Breakthrough: Whitlam in the Middle Kingdom, 1971.

Eric Knight is a senior lecturer in innovation and management at the University of Sydney Business School. He is the author of Why We Argue About Climate Change, which was nominated for the 2014 John Button Prize, and Reframe: How to Solve the World's Trickiest Problems. He previously worked for the Boston Consulting Group and studied at Oxford University as a Rhodes Scholar.

Noel Pearson is a lawyer and activist and the chairman of the Cape York Partnership. He has published many essays and newspaper articles, and is the author of Up from the Mission and Radical Hope.

SUBSCRIBE to Quarterly Essay & SAVE over 25% on the cover price

Subscriptions: Receive a discount and never miss an issue. Mailed direct to your door.

- ☐ **1 year subscription** (4 issues): $59 within Australia incl. GST. Outside Australia $89.
- ☐ **2 year subscription** (8 issues): $105 within Australia incl. GST. Outside Australia $165.

* All prices include postage and handling.

Back Issues: (Prices include postage and handling.)

- ☐ **QE 2** ($15.99) John Birmingham *Appeasing Jakarta*
- ☐ **QE 4** ($15.99) Don Watson *Rabbit Syndrome*
- ☐ **QE 6** ($15.99) John Button *Beyond Belief*
- ☐ **QE 7** ($15.99) John Martinkus *Paradise Betrayed*
- ☐ **QE 8** ($15.99) Amanda Lohrey *Groundswell*
- ☐ **QE 10** ($15.99) Gideon Haigh *Bad Company*
- ☐ **QE 11** ($15.99) Germaine Greer *Whitefella Jump Up*
- ☐ **QE 12** ($15.99) David Malouf *Made in England*
- ☐ **QE 13** ($15.99) Robert Manne with David Corlett *Sending Them Home*
- ☐ **QE 14** ($15.99) Paul McGeough *Mission Impossible*
- ☐ **QE 15** ($15.99) Margaret Simons *Latham's World*
- ☐ **QE 17** ($15.99) John Hirst *"Kangaroo Court"*
- ☐ **QE 18** ($15.99) Gail Bell *The Worried Well*
- ☐ **QE 19** ($15.99) Judith Brett *Relaxed & Comfortable*
- ☐ **QE 20** ($15.99) John Birmingham *A Time for War*
- ☐ **QE 21** ($15.99) Clive Hamilton *What's Left?*
- ☐ **QE 22** ($15.99) Amanda Lohrey *Voting for Jesus*
- ☐ **QE 23** ($15.99) Inga Clendinnen *The History Question*
- ☐ **QE 24** ($15.99) Robyn Davidson *No Fixed Address*
- ☐ **QE 25** ($15.99) Peter Hartcher *Bipolar Nation*
- ☐ **QE 26** ($15.99) David Marr *His Master's Voice*
- ☐ **QE 27** ($15.99) Ian Lowe *Reaction Time*
- ☐ **QE 28** ($15.99) Judith Brett *Exit Right*
- ☐ **QE 29** ($15.99) Anne Manne *Love & Money*
- ☐ **QE 30** ($15.99) Paul Toohey *Last Drinks*
- ☐ **QE 31** ($15.99) Tim Flannery *Now or Never*
- ☐ **QE 32** ($15.99) Kate Jennings *American Revolution*
- ☐ **QE 33** ($15.99) Guy Pearse *Quarry Vision*
- ☐ **QE 34** ($15.99) Annabel Crabb *Stop at Nothing*
- ☐ **QE 36** ($15.99) Mungo MacCallum *Australian Story*
- ☐ **QE 37** ($15.99) Waleed Aly *What's Right?*
- ☐ **QE 38** ($15.99) David Marr *Power Trip*
- ☐ **QE 39** ($15.99) Hugh White *Power Shift*
- ☐ **QE 42** ($15.99) Judith Brett *Fair Share*
- ☐ **QE 43** ($15.99) Robert Manne *Bad News*
- ☐ **QE 44** ($15.99) Andrew Charlton *Man-Made World*
- ☐ **QE 45** ($15.99) Anna Krien *Us and Them*
- ☐ **QE 46** ($15.99) Laura Tingle *Great Expectations*
- ☐ **QE 47** ($15.99) David Marr *Political Animal*
- ☐ **QE 48** ($15.99) Tim Flannery *After the Future*
- ☐ **QE 49** ($15.99) Mark Latham *Not Dead Yet*
- ☐ **QE 50** ($15.99) Anna Goldsworthy *Unfinished Business*
- ☐ **QE 51** ($15.99) David Marr *The Prince*
- ☐ **QE 52** ($15.99) Linda Jaivin *Found in Translation*
- ☐ **QE 53** ($15.99) Paul Toohey *That Sinking Feeling*
- ☐ **QE 54** ($15.99) Andrew Charlton *Dragon's Tail*

Payment Details: I enclose a cheque/money order made out to Schwartz Publishing Pty Ltd. Please debit my credit card (Mastercard or Visa accepted).

Card No. ☐☐☐☐ ☐☐☐☐ ☐☐☐☐ ☐☐☐☐

Expiry date /

CCV

Amount $

Cardholder's name

Signature

Name

Address

Email

Phone

Post or fax this form to: Quarterly Essay, Reply Paid 79448, Collingwood VIC 3066 / Tel: (03) 9486 0288 / Fax: (03) 9486 0244 / Email: subscribe@blackincbooks.com Subscribe online at **www.quarterlyessay.com**

www.ingramcontent.com/pod-product-compliance
Lightning Source LLC
Chambersburg PA
CBHW081402270326
41930CB00015B/3388